Contents

CW00847032

About the author

Nick has over 30 years' experience in Business Management and Communications. From work with clients such as Army Recruiting Group, BSkyB, Abbey National, Avis Fleet, Securicor, Eastern Electricity, BAA Gatwick, Polygram, Oxfam Publishing, Government Computing and West Midlands Police, Nick has a broad understanding of business growth strategies.

Nick is particularly pleased with the work undertaken to:-

1. Brand Gatwick as London Gatwick - Building International relationships.
2. Build the B2B database for AVIS Fleet - Identifying Growth businesses.
3. Build the MIS System for Army Recruiting Group – Running Government Business.
4. Develop the engagement strategy for West Midlands Police – Community Engagement.
5. Promote the Small Business Rate Relief Campaign – Roll out a National Campaign.
6. Combat *Churn* for BSkyB – Targeted mapping Campaign – Geo Demographics.

Prior to founding the Agency in 1988 Nick was group accountant for *Collett Dickenson Pearce's* below the line Agency RSVP Group. Nick also helped build a public house group from 3 to 15 pubs in 3 years and has worked in financial services for Flemings Bank.

Nick is an experienced trainer, facilitator and workshop leader. He has participated in Executive Education programmes as a student and as a tutor. He holds a degree in Pure Physics from London University, worked with Gary Hamel at London Business School on Change Management and Strategy Implementation on the 1996 Exec MBA course and has been facilitating change ever since.

His specialities include:- Customer Understanding, Customer Engagement, Internal and External Change Management, Customer led incremental Innovation, Brand led Fundamental Innovation, Building Inspiration through Belief and Trust, Empowerment whilst keeping track of activities and ROI.

Nick is currently Chair of Welwyn Hatfield Chamber of Commerce.

Introduction

I have written this book for all the amazing people whose livelihoods are currently, or are about to become, dependent upon their wits and hard work. That is, those of you who are reviewing an existing business or starting a new one. Be it your first or twenty first venture, this book is designed to help and support you on your journey.

If you are brave enough to take the step into business, you deserve all the help you can get. If you value your business and those who love you, this book is for you.

I was fortunate enough to start running my own businesses in my mid-twenties, which means that I now have some 30 years' experience of the joy and exhilaration of getting it right and the loneliness and frustration of getting it wrong.

This experience tells me that learning to run a business is a bit like learning to ride a motorcycle, rewarding and exhilarating when you get it right, but painful and potentially dangerous when you get it wrong.

My overriding objective in writing this book is to help you succeed by :-

1. Identifying the likely future challenges for your business.
2. Thinking through with you, which skills you have, and which you need to find.
3. Finding you those support skills before you encounter the challenge.
4. Ensuring that you are prepared for the challenges you may encounter.
5. Stopping you taking the wrong advice, that could cost you your business.

I have thought long and hard about my own businesses and the manner in which, full of youthful enthusiasm, I ran headlong into various traps. This book shares with you some of those experiences. If I had my time again, I would have sought out more real business people with real business experience and the right contacts. If I had met those people earlier, they could have helped to steer me through the maze, leaving me free to grow my businesses.

There are three themes that run through the book that are designed to protect you and provide you with a guiding light when you need it.

Those themes are:-

1. **The *WHY?* - WHY you are in business**

    WHY your business is a *Force for Good.*
    WHY your staff and customers should believe in what you do and support you in good times and bad.

2. **The *WHAT?* – WHAT you do today**

    WHAT you do to generate cash.
    WHAT you do today to keep your staff, customers and suppliers happy.
    WHAT you do to maximise your gross profit.

    and

3. **The *HOW?* - HOW you will build a better tomorrow.**

   HOW your staff, customers and suppliers support your vision and make it their own.
   HOW you build the right team around you – **You are not alone.**
   HOW you define the stepping stones to reach your vision of a better world.
   HOW you engage with your customers to understand their changing needs.
   HOW you empower your staff to develop the skills to deliver against those needs.
   HOW you continuously reinvent yourself.
   HOW you build a skills base that lets you drive the agenda by being a thought leader.
   HOW you ensure that your thought leadership aligns with *WHY* you are in Business.

Some 90% of UK start-up businesses fail, 50% in the first 2 years - I don't want you to be one of them.

This is not the sole preserve of start-ups. 80% established businesses fail within 10 years, and there are some very predictable reasons. My first business survived for over 10 years, and I have the scars to prove it. I will share some of those experiences with you.

I will try to show you how the quantifying and measuring aspects of your business, the systems and accounts, can provide guidance to the human elements that actually make things happen.

I will show also you how aligning the values of your brand *The WHY – The Force for Good*, with the current, future and evolving, needs of your staff and customers, will build a community that wants to be part of your success.

In this manner you can all join in the evolving reality, of the steps towards your shared vision. This evolutionary process is one of continual learning. There is a cycle of engage, learn, grow and repeat.

This is how you remain relevant in a changing world and ensure your business thrives and survives.

At this point I would like to acknowledge that there are many people out there better placed to help you than I. So, in each chapter I will try to put you in touch with an expert in your required area. You will be able to consider their suitability by reading their e-books to see what they have done and that they understand your issues. Their e-books may well help you solve your problem, but if they don't you can either contact myself or the authors for more detail, should you need to do so. Always remember -

You are not alone.

To this end, my team are building a network of experienced business people, who have demonstrated their skills by producing their own books which have been vetted and vouched for by Chamber members. If you feel that you can help other people's businesses to thrive, please get in touch with me on nick@welhatchamber.co.uk .

As you will see throughout the book I am inviting you join up with existing communities, so you can build your own. I revisit this in the final chapter, but for the minute let's get on with building your business.

May the Force for Good be with You!

Reader Guidance

When should you read this book?

This book is designed to be kept by your bedside and on your mobile phone, so whether you are planning your next ¼'s activity, trying to think through a particular problem or just looking for a source of ideas, you can pick it up, read the relevant chapter and, where necessary, find some help.

How to use this book

The book has been structured to help you identify, which challenges you are likely to encounter next, what might be involved and if you would like some guidance, where to find it.

The chapters have been set out in the order of the types of challenges, or growth stages, you are likely to encounter. Each chapter has four sections:-

1. Some often asked **Questions**, a checklist, to see what you know and what you don't.
2. Some things to **Think About**, to help you identify likely challenges.
3. Some **Sources of Help,** access to people, often authors, that we know, and online sources of information.
4. Some **Further Reading,** links to books we recommend.

Scan the Questions and see if they apply to your current or future plans. If they do, read on, if not, skip to the next chapter.

I will have succeeded when you can say:-

I understand my current growth stage.

I understand the potential challenges.

I know the skills I have on my team and where the gaps are.

I know when and where to find the skills to fill those gaps.

Where your questions remain unanswered, please contact me on nick@welhatchamber.co.uk and where appropriate we will try to source someone to help you, or to write an e-book addressing your concerns.

Specialist terms are shown in *Italics* and are explained in the **Glossary of Terms** at the end of this book.

Introducing George

Periodically you will come across George.

> **George Says**
> **"Remember This"**

George is our mutual friend. He provides some "Take Home" or more accurately "Take to Work" thoughts that are designed to give you a phrase that embodies certain concepts.

As you build your teams you can use these phrases to describe a sphere of *Shared Knowledge* and learning within the team.

Acknowledgements

I would like to express my thanks to my wife Lynn my daughter Melanie and all my friends and colleagues that I have learned with along the way, in particular all the staff I have grown with, the customers we have shared success with, The Welwyn and Hatfield Chamber of Commerce, Gary Hamel from London Business School and my friends who have helped with this book, Carl French, David Gill, Jonathan Harradine, Morgana Evans, Neil Deuchar and Steve Harris for the excellent cartoons characters which I hope will make you smile.

Review

'You are never too young or too old to learn and should never take your eyes off the ball when it comes to planning, developing and running your business. This applies at every stage of its development. There are numerous help guides covering every aspect of business development but 'Thrive and Survive in Business' is a step by step guide which is set apart from most by the light yet positive touch with which it is written. Supported by the authors' extensive (over 30 years) and ever developing business experience in the management and expansion of businesses. A succinct warning as to the pitfalls and mishaps that can occur and what action to take, bearing in mind that the CUSTOMER is always at the centre of your plans. Keep it in the top drawer of your desk, on your bedside table and on your computer- in other words always ensure you have it to hand to refer to in times of need'.

Tim Collins

Tim Collins has a reputation for highly creative solutions to brand and business development throughout a long and successful career in management and planning:

Marketing Management and Planning- Reckitt and Coleman, Imperial Tobacco and Sutton Seeds.

Agency Management and Planning - Aalders and Marchant, Ogilvy and Mather Partners and Saatchi and Saatchi.

Chapter 1 – Being a Business Owner – The Reality

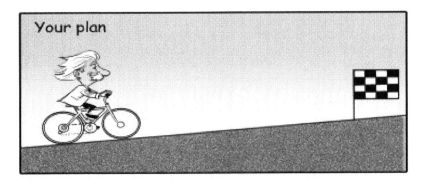

Learning how to negotiate the pitfalls, at each growth stage, is all part of the challenge of being in business. If you know in advance that you are going to need a mountain bike, a ladder, a canoe and an umbrella, it feels like an adventure, if not it can be daunting. A crystal ball is always helpful.

Successful businesses don't necessarily have all the skills, but they do know which challenges are coming up, and where to find the necessary skills to address those challenges - which is pretty close to having a crystal ball.

Arthur Ashe, the Wimbledon tennis champion, who went on to a very successful consulting career, said :-

> *"Start where you are*
> *Use what you have*
> *Do what you can"*

From 30 odd years of being in business it is clear to me that business owners are often so busy chasing the next sale to pay the bills, that they don't know their business's current growth stage.   As a result, they are unprepared for the next challenge.

This can easily turn an adventure into an assault course. One is enjoyable, the other is not.

So let's start out on this journey by preparing ourselves for what is coming next.

Start where you are

Whichever growth stage you are currently experiencing, always start with your guiding light, namely **WHY** you started the business in the first place - your values and your vision. Your belief in these is vital, because it is how you will align the values of your brand *The Force for Good*, with those of your staff and customers, to ensure that you are all pulling together, in the same shared direction.

When you start out, you are driving the business. Over time your business will take on a life and identity of its own. It will become more than the sum of all its parts. For this to happen it is important that all those parts share common goals. As we shall see, this is how you ensure your business thrives and survives in rough seas.

The following diagram sets out some typical business growth stages in your business where you are likely to encounter challenges.

These growth stages are represented in the content of Chapters 2 to 11 of this book.

Take a few minutes to think about the current growth stages in your business. Where are you today?

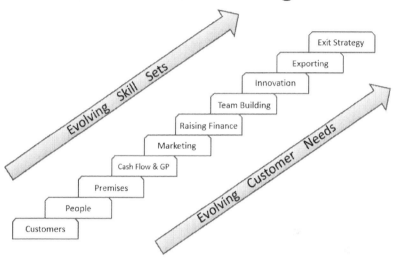

What are you thinking about in the evening and when you wake in the morning? What is on your mind? What is helping you build your vision, and where are the stumbling blocks?

Write these down, as the things that are currently demanding your attention are probably your current growth stages, then refer to the relevant chapter. At each stage try to answer the question "Why are we doing this?"

We are "team builders" because we believe...

Growth Stages are areas of your businesses where you take stock of the likely upcoming challenges, see if you are prepared and have the necessary skills and if not, regroup before proceeding.

Never forget that part of the reason for starting a business is to improve the lot of your friends and family. It is the job of the business to generate the cash to make your dreams achievable. A nice house, a personal workshop. The things that are for your family are separate from those that are for your business. Do not confuse the two, it will cloud your judgement.

Use what you have

WHAT you have, is your judgement. You decide where your resources of *Time, Skills* and *Cash* are spent. What your staff do, for which customers, to generate cash today. In short, it is a balancing act.

People say that businesses fail because they run out of cash. I would say they fail because they are not generating enough cash. More specifically because they run out of time to get it right.

There is a time in every business owner's life when you are on top of things and you feel supported. You feel great. Then, as your world gets more complex, you run out of the time and energy to solve everything. It simply catches up with you. This is the point at which you need to seek help, and the sooner the better. It is perfectly possible to avoid potential problems, you just have to see them coming and give yourself time to work out how to steer round them.

Another thing I often come across is business owners who cannot solve a particular issue and believe that their problems are unique. They are often embarrassed that they cannot solve them, and so they just carry on running out of time. The good news is that very few problems have not been come across before. You just need to recognise the problem and find the right person to ask. A problem shared is a problem halved.

I have illustrated this using *The Waterwheel Model*. I want to keep you on the right side, the supported or Green side of the *Waterwheel.*

The Waterwheel Model

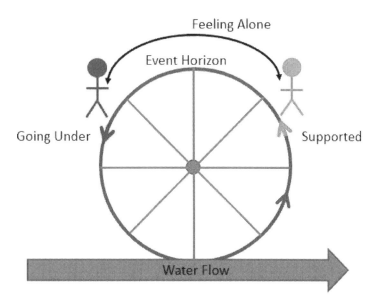

The *Waterwheel* shows the typical balancing act that all business owners experience as their business grows. The more plates you spin, the more you need the right support to keep those plates spinning. At this point you are the Green Man on the right.

As you know, it does not take much for some of those plates to start to wobble and then you have to rush around to bring them up to speed again. This is when you can feel alone. When you do, it is vital that you get the right help from the right people, and get that help quickly. If you don't get that help or you delay, it is all too easy for the wobbling plates to start falling, and you become the **Red Man**. There is most definitely an *Event Horizon* after which the waterwheel starts to pull you under.

When you are playing catch up, it can be too late for you to do anything about it.

> **Remember - You are not alone.**

To take a medical analogy.

In the *Waterwheel* model you start out as the Green Man on the right hand side, being supported. You know there are things you cannot deal with, and you would act straightaway, except that you cannot find the right help. This book helps you recognise the symptoms and diagnose the problem, so you can get the right help, before the problem becomes acute. Prevention is better than a cure and it allows you to concentrate on growing your business.

Inaction, or worse still a misdiagnosis from an inexperienced consultant, can turn you into the Red Man very quickly. Be extremely wary of self-appointed experts, with no business experience, who are dangerous and can severely damage the health of your business.

> **Find the Right Help –**
> **You are not Alone.**

Do what you can

This is **HOW** you inspire both your staff and your customers to be *Thought Leaders*, to stay ahead of the fashion curve, to understand what your customers want now and work with them to develop what they want in the future.

Product GP falls over time

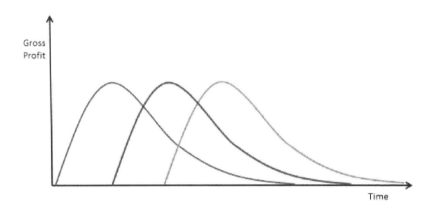

The key point here is that every product and service has its day in a given market. As new players come into the market and compete on price, or the market simply matures, the profit margins fall. In the ever faster changing world in which we live this happens increasingly quickly. One of the main reasons for business failure is the inability to change with the times. They simply become obsolete. I also think that business owners know this, because they see it in their accounts. They just don't know what to do about it. One answer is to build a business that has change built into its core brand values.

> ### *Have Fun! – Reinvent Yourself.*

It is worth mentioning early on that successful organisations often have two things in common.

1. The good fortune to be in the right place at the right time. (It is easy to be too soon or too late, if the customers don't want your product it will not sell) and

2. Access to a broad range of skills from the outset.

You need to have the following skills covered :-

The **WHY** – The Values and Vision - The Belief.
 – An Entrepreneur.

The **WHAT** – Someone who can produce what you are selling today
 – A Technician leading production staff.

The **HOW** – How to build the skills to design products for tomorrow
 – Staff and Customers with a *Shared Vision*.

You will also need access to the following people :-

Experienced business people with the skills to cover the following areas :- Sales, Recruitment, Property, Money, Marketing, Teambuilding, Innovation and finding New Markets.

Some thoughts on the development phases of your business.

Status	Mind Sets	Skillset	Timeframe	Activity	Outputs
Start Where you are	**WHY?**	Thought Leadership Entrepreneur Vision Shaping Markets Innovator	Belief in Today's Vision of the Future & Long term Brand Building	Team Building Shared vision of the Future	Belief in a better future
Use What you have	**WHAT?**	Revenue Leadership Generating Demand	Knowledge of Today's Customer Needs	Delivering high quality customer solutions that solve today's problems Pays today's bills	Trust Today = Platform for future Growth
Do What you can	**HOW?**	Brand Leadership Changing Perceptions	Understanding of Tomorrow's Customer Needs	Building relationship with your clients and their customers	Trust for Tomorrow – High GP %'s

---

A Success Story

A friend of mine was asked

"How do you keep all those plates spinning? Do you have a Crystal Ball?"

He replied

"No Crystal ball, but I know which three plates I need to keep spinning and I trust the people spinning the other plates"

It is worth remembering that when you get that feeling in the top of your stomach that says "I don't know where the money is coming from to pay the wages next month or the month after", that this is perfectly normal.

It is connected to knowing when to brake and when to accelerate out of a bend.

It is that feeling that time is precious, that somehow you are in a race, where you cannot see your competitors, but you know they are there.

It is how you know that you and your team are a dynamic, living thriving community, and that what you are doing is worthwhile.

In summary, it is how you know that you are *A Force for Good* – because you care!

The following chapters explore the skills areas mentioned above in more detail by looking at the things you need to consider at each business growth stage. I do not think that all businesses go through the same growth stages in the same order, they don't. However, I do know that many business owners experience problems in these areas at some stage of their careers.

So let's have a look at the first stage of business, having a customer.

Sources of help

Visit http://www.welhatchamber.co.uk/thrive-and-survive to access a continually updated web page of useful links.

Further reading

The Smart Startup – *John Elder*

The E-Myth Revisited: Why Most Small Businesses Don't Work – *Michael Gerber*

The Slight Edge: Turning Simple Disciplines into Massive Success and Happiness - *Jeff Olson*

The Effective Executive: The Definitive Guide to Getting the Right Things Done - *Peter F. Drucker*

Arthur Ashe on Tennis - *Arthur Ashe*

Chapter 2 – Customers

Sales start before your salesman calls!

This is how your customers think about you. The first and most important skill required to run a scalable business is being able to see your business through the eyes of your customers.

The first stage of being in business is to have paying customers.

"Although your customers won't love you if you give bad service, your competitors will".   Kate Zabriskie

Look after your customers
and they will look after you.

Why do *Customers* come first in this book?

I have often been asked:

"Surely you need Staff, Working Capital and a Premises before you start a business?"

Be very careful not to fall into this first trap. How do you know what your customers want? Or, when they might be ready for your products? The relevant test is, to find customers ready to pay for your services. Market research is one level of certainty, people parting with their hard earned cash is another. This book spells out that you should not start a business until you have paying customers, the profits from whom, you can use to build your business.

90% of businesses fail, 50% of them within 2 years, because that is how long it takes to exhaust the business owner's savings and assets. Do not join that long line of people who have been advised to take that path by unscrupulous or worse still - ill-informed "Advisors".

So you need to start with Customers.

Wherever your customers come from, be they cash customers in the local market or mobile customers buying your phone App, they are all customers and they all need to be understood. In fact, more accurately you need to understand what your customers want from a relationship with your business, that is - their *Customer Needs*.

Have a think about the following questions. If you really know the answers, well done!

If not read on:-

Questions

1. What is a customer?
2. Where do I find new customers?
3. Who are my most profitable customers?
4. Am I over reliant upon one customer?
5. Why do my customers buy from me?
6. How can I choose the best customers?
7. Which customers will help me grow my business?
8. Which customers will make my business more secure, exciting, fun and less risky?

Think About

What is a customer?

Before I try to answer this question, I need to introduce a concept that will tell you:-

1. How important a customer is to your business financially.
2. How much they value their relationship with your business.
3. How much you should spend to keep them happy.
4. How loyal they are to your business.
5. How likely they are to help you develop new products - The future of your business.
6. How much your business is worth?
7. How successful you are when compared to your competitors.
8. When it is time to look for new markets for old products.
9. Your profitability.

So it is an important concept. In the introduction to the book I said that I would show you how the quantifying and measuring aspects of your business, the systems and accounts, can provide guidance to the human elements that actually make things happen.

So hold tight because here comes the big one - *Gross Profit*.

What is Gross Profit (GP)?

Let's suppose, for example, that you are a baker. You sell cakes. Your gross profit is the money you make from the sale of each cake. Gross profit is your sales, less those costs directly associated with making a cake, typically the materials and labour used to make the cake.

So your Gross Profit for selling a cake might be:-

Selling Price		£5.00
Direct Costs or Cost of Sales		
Eggs, Flower, Icing, Jam	£1.00	
Gas for the Oven	£0.50	
Labour of the Baker	£1.00	

		£2.50
		=====
Gross Profit		£2.50

This gives a Gross Profit of £2.50
which as a % of sales = £2.50 / 5.00 = 50% = the Gross Profit %.

This number is important for two reasons:-

Firstly, it represents your contribution to overhead.

Your overheads are :-

Admin	**Establishment**	**Sales**	**&**	**Finance costs**.
Telephones	*Rent and Rates*	*Advertising*		*Bank Charges*.

Overhead costs have nothing to do with the costs of baking your cake. They also are reasonably fixed. So let us say that your overheads are £2,500 a month, then you will have to sell 1,000 cakes a month to break even (1000 * £2.50 = £2500). Which given 25 working days in a month is 40 cakes a day.

> So now you know that if you sell 60 cakes a day you will make a profit before tax (PBT) of £1,250 a month. So 60*25=1500 cakes sold, so sales will be £7,500.   With a GP% of 50% = £3,750 GP, less your overhead of £2,500 leaves a PBT of £1,250.

This is how you should think of your business. This is the quantifiable systems side of your business. How does this relate to your customers, staff and brand values?

And secondly it tells you how important you are to your customers when compared to your competitors.

Suppose you were in business to create the most beautiful cakes in the world, cakes that made people smile, cakes they have their photos taken next to. Cakes that enhanced people status and made them feel good about themselves. Suppose you sold wedding cakes to the rich and famous, cakes that had to outshine the wedding dress and be the focal point of the couples' future happiness as they cut your cake together and the cameras flash.

> What would such a cake be worth? More than £5? More than £50? More than £500? You might easily pay £1000 for such a cake.

> What would that do to your Gross Profit? Well it might be 10 times the materials = £10 and three times the gas, say £1.50 and OK a lot more time say £100, for 10 hours at £10 per hour. So your cost of sales is £111.50 with sales at £1000, your GP is now £888.50 = 89% GP.   So now if you bake three cakes a month you will make a small profit.

The point being that your skill levels and reputation enhance the price customers are happy to pay. This not only determines your GP%, it determines how many cakes you have to bake, how many hours you have to work and to which parties you are invited.

"*Gross Profit is an important number because it tells you how much your customers care about you.*"

So back to **What is a customer?** This is actually quite a big question. Let's continue with the bakery analogy. What types of customers do you have?

1. The passing trade who buy their bread – We all need to eat.
2. The passing trade who buy cakes – We all need a treat.
3. The lunchtime trade – Office workers looking for a sandwich.
4. The cup of coffee trade – People in search of a chat.
5. Builders after an all-day breakfast – Stocking up for the day's work.
6. Regular special occasions, birthdays etc. – A chance to show you care.
7. Big occasions – Births, weddings, funerals – Opportunities to celebrate success.

As you can see, each customer is defined by what he wants from a relationship with your business. We call these *"Customer Needs"*.

Each of these customer types are target markets, you might look at them as individuals or groups of people. I would suggest the following approach.

1. Start with the messages, what do you want to say to them? Convenient, Local, Friendly, Home Made, Fresh Produce, Welcoming, etc.
2. What is the method of communications *The media,* In Store, Posters, Local Paper, Local radio, Magazines, National Press, TV, email, Direct mail, Social, aeroplane fly-past banners or a Spiderman suit with a placard. It is a long list.
3. Then think about your GP. Which groups are returning which GP%'s, the higher the GP the more targeted the messages and the more you might be prepared to spend.

Then group your customers together into target markets where the GP determines the media you can afford to use, and the messages are firstly media determined and then campaign determined. So now you know what you are saying to whom, and what each message costs.

The next consideration here is how loyal are your customers, generally customers are grouped in the following manner

- **Suspects:** People you suspect might be interested in your products.
- **Prospects:** People who have expressed an interest but are not yet customers.
- **Customers:** People who pay you money.
- **Advocates:** People who tell their friends how wonderful you are.

Interestingly the more customers are loyal to you, the higher the GP% they are happy to pay because they understand and appreciate the value you give them. If this value is Status, you can get to the point where the more they pay the higher their status.

There are many examples of this from Lady Diana's Wedding Dress, designed by David and Elisabeth Emanuel, presumably demand for their talents increased significantly after the wedding was broadcast across the world.

To the more day to day example of Heinze baked beans, people pay a 50% premium over stores own brand, just to have Heinze written on the tin. This is pure status and demonstrates the value of a brand.

We are however, straying into the realms of marketing here, but hopefully that sheds some light on what a customer means to your business.

Finding new customers

Customers will buy from you today:-

1. When they understand **The WHY** – *The Force for Good.* When they know you, trust you, believe in you and want to support you – It is all about relationships.
2. When they value **The WHAT** – When you deliver the right mix of price, convenience, quality, choice and customer experience for their needs today.
3. When they feel **The HOW** – How they can be part of your vision and trust you to be the guardian of their future style well-being and influence, and
4. When they are good and ready, and not before.

Consider:-

Looking for new customers is about finding groups of people who aspire to your values.

1.   Where do your existing customers come from?
2.   Are you part of their future aspirations?
3.   Do you share common goals?
4.   Does your team share those common goals?
5.   How are you communicating this? Externally and Internally?

Finding new customers is important because existing customers move on.

New customers are the lifeblood of your business.

A Success Story

I have talked about the importance of a shared vision and shared values, thanks to my staff, and the vast majority of the clients we had, those beliefs shone out of the Agency.

This meant that potential customers and staff wanted to work with us. In fact they would compete to join our learning organisation. This meant that customers were happy to pay extra and almost cherish us as their Agency, and staff were happy to go the extra mile, often half the night, to get the best work they possible could out there.

The most profitable customers

1. Within a particular market sector, the Wedding Dress market for example, the amount your customer is prepared to pay, does not depend upon you or your product – it does depend on how you make them feel – it is about their perception of their status as a result of their relationship with your brand. It really is, all about them.
2. They will be those customers whose status is enhanced by their relationship with your brand.
3. You must know who and how much. Your *Gross Profit* is the most important number.
4. You need to measure gross profit. Be it on the back of an envelope, in a spreadsheet or via a job costing system, it is important to know how much you make on each sale.
5. Not knowing the gross profit on each sale puts your business and livelihood at risk.

Identifying your most profitable customer is important because they help you identify the types of people who value you the most, so you can look after them and find more of the same.

Your Gross Profit is the measure of how well your core values of **WHY, WHAT** *and* **HOW** *are perceived by your customers.*

A Cautionary Tale

My Agency was founded in 1989 just as targeted database marketing was taking off, (You have to get the timing right, I was lucky) and we had a gross profit after all direct salaries of 43% for the first 6 years of the business. I then watched those margins erode over time, and did not know what to do about it. The business was growing like topsy, but the margins were on the slide. A very dangerous combination.

I thought of all sorts of reasons why this was happening, but I fundamentally believed that the good times would return. In fact they were gone for the foreseeable future and those kind of margins are a thing of the past in the industry to this day. The point being that I simply did not know what to do about it.

What I should have done was Re-invented myself. So who should I have asked? My advisors were a High Street Bank's Threadneedle Street branch, another in Hatton Garden, a top four firm of accountants central London office, a top ten firm of international lawyers, in fact we had several firms of lawyers on the books, and the full range of London Business School's Professors.

All of the above were very clever people at the top of their professions, but I can tell you now, that none of them helped me find the answers I was looking for. The answer was that, not only our marketing niche but, the whole industry had had its day. The smart move, with the benefit of hindsight, would have been a switch into mobile phones.

The people who did know were other businessmen. Some tried to tell me, but I did not listen, because I did not know where their advice fitted. I had not understood that we were at the "Innovation needed" stage of the business growth stages.

> **You are not Alone.**
>
> *Mix with other business people so you can reinvent yourself.*

There are good guys out there; you just have to find them. This is why I am building our group of advisors with real experience that you can access through our Sources of Help and Further Reading sections.

Over reliance on one customer

1. *"I am your biggest customer"* means "Give me a better deal".
2. This does not have to mean money, in fact it should not. It may mean a better service.

Knowing whether or not you are over reliant on one customer is important because if they do leave you can lose good staff that you have trained for years. You also have a responsibility to those staff.

A Cautionary Tale

One of my businesses worked for many years for an innovative event management company and handled the databases and marketing for their events at Earls Court in London. They successfully sold their business to a major publishing group who own a National newspaper. One of the client's senior people took some bad marketing decisions, and we were asked by the client to do more work for half the price. I am beginning to think the man was an accountant!!

We said no, they moved the business elsewhere, the firm they moved to promptly lost all their data and went bust. Not good for anyone. Some of our staff had to find new jobs, as we were over reliant on one client in that part of the business.

This must have cost the client a few million pounds. They bought a perfectly good business and ruined it in 9 months.

> *Watch out when your customers are bought out or when your clients contacts move jobs.*

Why do my customers buy from me?

This is an important question, because the answer will drive some of your marketing. You also need to know that the reasons can change quite quickly. One of the ways to track these changes is to monitor your *Gross Profit* by product sector. When you spot your GP% dropping, which in time it will, you will know that your *Customer Needs* are evolving, and it is time to find out why. One of the techniques used to stay ahead of that particular curve is to use *Net Promoter Scores.*

See *Net Promoter Scores* in **Chapter 6 – Marketing**.

> *If you don't know why your customers buy from you, what are you going to tell new customers about your business?*

How do I choose the best customers?

Your best customers will be those that see you as a business partner rather than a supplier. Those customers who make you compete on price should be avoided, they are bad for morale and your GP%.

You can choose your best customers by building a reputation for being passionate about your chosen sphere of operations and seeing who wants to help you reach your goals.

Our best customers were always those who shared our vision and aspirations. Our worst felt as if they lived in windowless offices, and were out for what they could get.

> **"A Creative man is motivated by the desire to achieve, not by the desire to beat others."**
>
> **Ayn Rand**

Which customers will help me grow my business?

Those customers with *Common Aims*.

It is important to have an understanding of what is happening in yours and your clients' sectors. That way your clients will know that you care about their future, and they in turn will care about yours.

Have a look at your diary; who are you spending time with? People who know about your market, or the bottom feeders?

Once you know which customers share a common goal, you will know who to contact and why they should do business with you.

A Success Story

When David Ogilvy, founder of Ogilvy and Mather, was starting out in business, he was in the right place at the right time when he won the American Express account.

You certainly make your own luck, it's a numbers game. If you meet a lot of people some of them will be good for you. In the case of AMEX they were looking to expand their product into new markets and every time Amex launched in a new country, Ogilvy and Mather were able to open a new agency in that country.

> **Try to find businesses that are going places and share your passions and goals.**

Those customers that are looking for a long term relationship. Those that will encourage you to *Innovate* - They may also want the right mix of service and price for the certainty of cash flow.

Organisations that want the cheapest price all the time, are a risk to you and themselves. They are best given to your nearest competitor, so he can spend all his time servicing this demanding customer for little return, leaving you free to go after emerging players with a shared vision of the future.

This is about the spread of customers. You want some big established customers, some smaller innovative ones, so you can be connected to, and knowledgeable about, your sector.

You need to feel like a safe pair of hands.

Think about seasonality and the spread of customers to keep you busy all year.

It only takes two or three bad months to wipe out your profit for the year.

*If you can, be a **Thought Leader** – then you will be part of everyone's future.*

Sources of help

Visit http://www.welhatchamber.co.uk/thrive-and-survive to access a continually updated web page of useful links.

Further reading

Good To Great: Why Some Companies Make the Leap...And Others Don't - *Jim Collins*

Chapter 3 – Working with People

"What do you mean all those part time, Zero Hour contract people have left?? What happened to Staff Loyalty?"

> **Look after your People and They will look after you.**

"Choose a job you love, and you will never have to work a day in your life" Confucius

"I believe that if life gives you lemons, you should make lemonade... then try to find somebody whose life has given them vodka, and have a party." Ron White

It is difficult to grow your business on your own because it is constrained by your time. Ideally you should be able to do the things you are good at, and have someone else do the things you are not so good at, or do not require your skills.

So to grow a business you need a team with complementary skills and a shared vision of the future. Being in business allows you to get other people to earn money for you, but as we will see, managing staff can bring a range of potential problems.

Remember there are some excellent HR and Recruitments firms out there. I want to help you find the right resource for your business on terms that work for you.

*Employ people that believe in the same things that you do **The WHY.***

*So **WHAT** they do will keep todays customers happy, and*

***HOW** they do it will be customer focussed and help your business evolve with changing customer needs.*

Questions

1. How can I attract the best people?
2. Should I use a recruitment agency?
3. What about self-employed people?
4. What about links with Colleges and Universities?
5. Employing friends and family?
6. Am I over reliant on one member of staff?
7. Changing behaviour.
8. Employment contracts – Do I need a lawyer?
9. Staff security issues? Intellectual property – How does this work?

Think About

How can I attract the best people?

> *Get your Brand right and the good people will come to you.*

1. If you have a boring business proposition you will pay for the best. If you have an exciting proposition, the best will come to you.
2. Be VERY clear about **WHY** your business is a *Force for Good*. We do this *"Because we believe ......"*
3. Think about where you need help - Sales, Admin, Finance, IT, Management, and be clear about who does **WHAT**. What does success looks like and how can staff share in your beliefs?
    a) What is their part of the **WHY?**
    b) Manage the **WHAT?** in terms of outputs defined by *Key Performance Indicators KPI's.*
    c) Give freedom over the **HOW?** So staff have ownership of the *Shared Vision*.

A Success Story

There was a lovely story about President Kennedy visiting the Kennedy Space Centre and meeting a man with a mop cleaning the floor.

The President asked him *"What do you do here?"*

The man replied *"I am helping to put a man on the moon"*

Shared visions really matter.

He believed in the WHY.

---

4. Recruit the best you can get.
5. Go for the people with enthusiasm for their part in your shared vision. If you can feel that, employ them.

You need good staff to build good teams. With good teams, life is fun and your business grows.

So you see - You are not alone.

Should I use a recruitment agency?

1. There are many reasons to use recruitment agencies, as Debbie Glinnan of Parallel HR says "There are some good ones and some shockers". If you are looking for temporary staff or admin roles where you can afford to replace people, then fine, just watch out for those agencies that think that your staff belong to them. There is a very real danger that they will charge you to find a member of staff, let you train them up then sell your skills and knowledge on to one of your competitors.
2. Think about PR as a good recruitment tool. Linked In etc.
3. Be wary of HR consultants coming into your business. If they don't share your carefully constructed vision, they can do a great deal of damage.

*Be very clear about **WHAT** you want from your staff. Build other sources of new staff.*

If the only way to get the right staff is through your agency then insist on a three month rebate scheme. You cannot judge someone in one month.

DO NOT assume that the only way to get good staff is through your agency because then you will get what they give you.

A Cautionary Tale

In my advertising business we had a brand that was a force for good and people were knocking on the door to join. As is so often the case we had become a victim of our own success. We were winning business at a good rate and needed to find specialist staff to handle that business. We used a recruitment agency, with whom we had agreed an exclusivity clause (we would only use that agency) and a No Poaching agreement. (The recruitment agency would not approach the business's staff.)

Some two years later the recruitment agency was approaching the staff they had placed and other staff within our business, offering my staff better deals, more money etc. elsewhere. We found out, warned other people and stopped using the recruitment agency.

If you use a recruitment agency have a trusted member of staff on their books reporting to you.

If you employ someone who has worked before, phone the business owner and see if what he says agrees with the references supplied by your agency.

What about self-employed people?

1. Self-employed people are just that. They work for themselves. Their *Brand Vision* is theirs not yours.
2. They can be a very useful resource for addressing specific problems, a particular campaign, or project where you are buying in expertise or resource
3. Remember to maintain control of the project management and the client contact. It is your client and your project.
4. Remember to differentiate between consultants that look to train your staff in their ways, and those with real industry experience who can help with contacts and knowhow. Employ consultants with real business experience in your sector.

Self-employed people should be part of your change management program. Bring them in to light the path, ensure that knowledge transfer is part of their contract.

What about links with Colleges and Universities?

Consider apprentices versus graduate placement. Apprentices are a good way of building a home grown team with some longevity of employment at the right price. My personal experience of University placements was that the students gained a lot, but often did not stay.

The right links with academia can enhance your brand. Understand how academics operate. Work with the seasonal nature of their lives. Find the practical ones that want to engage with the outside world.

Employing friends and family?

Friends and Family? Consider the price if it does not work out.

Consider the effect on key players who are not family members.

In Chapter One, we talked about the reasons to keep your business and your immediate family separate to avoid conflicts of interest and confusions. There are examples of very successful family businesses, but in a world where you need to be increasingly quick on your feet, on balance I feel that family politics can only be an added complication.

Be very careful.

Am I over reliant on one member of staff?

This is a really tricky one because the more successful you are at delegating and growing your teams the more reliant you become.

I have talked about:-

- The WHY being your vision that you share with the team
- The WHAT being the things you have to deliver today, for your clients, to be in business, and
- The HOW being the domain of staff empowerment and customer led innovation.

The point about the HOW is that it is a *Shared Commodity*. It is the *Learning Organisation*.

The WHAT, is where you can manage your *Key Performance Indicators* (KPI's). By continuously moving the outputs upon which staff are assessed you can ensure that today's knowledge is continuously transferred to new members of the team.

This is how you manage over reliance. If you don't do this, you will only have yourself to blame.

This is a really important area.

> *If you find yourself being held to ransom – you are over reliant on that individual.*

Three Cautionary Tales

I can think of many occasions where staff output assessments did not run to plan. The reasons are normally connected with individual staff member's insecurities.

One lady was excellent until under pressure, when she was a complete liability, it turned out that she had a religious guilt ethic, and was terrified of failure. We reassured her that the team she was in would support her and it worked out.

Another lady was very thorough, hard-working and loyal, but whenever the task was remotely different she would stop the team moving forward. Her fear of the smallest unknown stopped the *Learning Organisation.* The team approach did not work. We should have parted company sooner than we did.

The worse scenarios I have come across are those individuals who want to build their own team, to the exclusion of others, within your organisation. These people are normally bullies, they try to stop other teams being successful because it shows them up. They intimidate people into being on their team and try to control everything. They then do nothing with the opportunity because they lack the talent or ambition. These people are dangerous, seek them out and get rid of them. Give them to your competitors as soon as you can.

Watch out for controlling rather than facilitating behaviour, cliques beginning to form in your business, previously happy members of staff being excluded and picked on.

This is one reason why Tesco's take their bright people and move them into different roles on a regular basis. It causes problems but it creates opportunities for the next tier of people to fill that space.

Changing behaviour

We are all creatures of habit. We know what we know and feel secure in that knowledge. We are in our comfort zones, when we have experienced the issues before and know how to handle them. If you ask someone to operate outside of their comfort zone, the brakes come on fast.

It does not matter what you say, you will encounter resistance. You have to encourage people to discover things for themselves. You have to *Facilitate Change*.

> *You change the way people think – by changing what they do.*

Once staff have found their own way of doing something, it will be part of their comfort zone. This is where teams can help, but it is important to have the right people on the team.

"Tell me and I forget, Teach me and I remember, Involve me and I Learn" Benjamin Franklyn

Please note. Team Building is covered in Chapter 8

The next point here is that you would like your staff to share your vision within their comfort zones. That is, they need their own vision, which has to do with shared values – **The WHY.**

You then want them to do things that are relevant to the needs of your customers - **The WHAT.**

And you need their youth, and hence understanding of emerging markets, and customer contacts to build a shared and evolving vision of the future of the organisation – **The HOW.**

A Success Story

One of my staff came from a family where no one had ever passed 11+ (a basic skills test taken at 11 years of age). She was keen and hard-working, and we ran a learning organisation, so we opened doors for her.

I am proud to say she went on to become group credit controller for a multi-national business and her daughter subsequently achieved a 2.1 Hons Degree from a good University.

Creating a *Learning Organisation* can give people the confidence to change their lives.

Employment contracts – Do I need a lawyer?

Yes. If you are employing people you should protect yourself, your staff and your business by having a clear agreement between you. The agreement should cater for future scenarios, whilst being clear but even handed. Understand why each clause exists. What does it achieve?

If you have a fair and even handed employment contract and a potential member of staff does not want to sign it or queries it too much, do not employ them. You cannot have different rules for different people. It is divisive and impossible to manage.

Employment Law is continuously changing.
Review your employment contracts annually.

> **Employment contracts put everyone on the same deal and avoid misunderstandings.**

Without this - How do you build trust?

Staff security issues? *Intellectual Property?*

This is a specialist area. The bottom line is that ideas had by people employed by you, or contracted to you working on behalf of your clients, must assign their copyright to you. Further, when they leave your organisation, they should have no rights to approach your clients or your staff, and any confidential information belonging to you or your clients must remain confidential.

Staff need to know that you are in charge.

You cannot have staff taking customers, IP or other staff, with them.

Sources of help

Debbie Glinnan Parallel HR - http://www.parallelhr.co.uk/

Longmores Employment Team - www.longmores-solicitors.co.uk/ site/services_business/employment_law/

Visit http://www.welhatchamber.co.uk/thrive-and-survive to access a continually updated web page of useful links.

Further reading

How to Employ your First 20 People - *Debbie Glinnan*

Fish!: A Remarkable Way to Boost Morale and Improve Results - *Stephen C. Lundin and John Christensen*

Who Moved My Cheese: An Amazing Way to Deal with Change in Your Work and in Your Life - *Johnson, Spencer*

Chapter 4 – Premises

"I'm loving it! It will cost you
a fortune to reassign your lease."

*"When it comes to property what you need is flexibility, and
hopefully the right Landlord"*

*"Do your own research. Properties that are not on the market can
still be available"*

OK this is a big one. After salary costs, premises costs are usually the next biggest cost to a business. If you sign up a 5 year lease you are stuck with that decision for 5 years and possibly more.

I have come across more real problems surrounding commercial property than any other area. I would try to find the right property people and invite them to be part of your team. You will need a surveyor and a lawyer. If you can, do business with them, introduce clients to them. Good property advice is essential.

The surveying profession has some great and generous people in it. The world of commercial property, however, has its fair share of sharp operators. *Caveat Emptor.*

Questions

1. Who should advise me?
2. How do I find out the right price?
3. What about business rates?
4. What are dilapidations?
5. Should I sign a personal guarantee?
6. Should I use a lawyer?
7. Can I trust my surveyor?
8. How do I find the right premises?
9. What about working from home?
10. Serviced offices / Hubs?

Think About

Who should advise me?

In the commercial property world, it is easy to take advice from the wrong person. The first thing you need to know is that anyone can call themselves a Surveyor. Those that are members of RICS the Royal Institution of Chartered Surveyors act within guidelines. RICS surveyors fall into two main camps. Surveyors who work for the landlord, who are often on a commission, and those who work for the tenant, normally called *Ratings Surveyors*. Those who claim to do both, particularly if their sign is outside the building, are normally working for the landlord.

> ***You must find the right advisor –***
> ***One who is on your side.***

How do I find the right premises?

Decide on a property type, size and a range of locations. Look around, pick an area. Visit existing tenants, ask what they are paying. Find out how long buildings remain empty. Decide upon how many square feet you are looking for. Write a letter to the occupiers of all the suitable buildings in the area, drop it off by hand and ask if anyone has spare capacity they would like to sub-let.

At the end of the day supply and demand will determine the price, make sure you have several options and play one off against the other. This will typically be your second highest business cost after salaries, you will also be tied in for several years, so try to get it right.

> ***A Premises can be a Boon –***
> ***Or a Millstone.***
>
> ***Get it Right.***

How do I find out the right price?

If a surveyor finds you the ideal property, only offers one choice, and tells you it is a rising market and there is a shortage of this type of property, then either he is working for the landlord or you might be looking in the wrong place. Just because a property is not on the market does not mean there is no deal to be done.

The right price is the best price you can negotiate, having done your research, found a number of suitable properties, (even if one is a *Stalking Horse)* and played one off against another. Don't forget that the landlord and his team will be playing exactly the same game as you and they do it for a living. Also remember that it is expensive, disruptive and time consuming to move. Landlords know this and will use it against you at the next rent review. So go for long rent reviews and be prepared to move.

If there genuinely is a shortage of similar properties in the area, supply and demand again, it may well be that the landlord can find a tenant prepared to pay a premium for your premises. Be mindful of this and if you are bluffing, make sure you have heads of agreement lined up on a new premises as you might well be asked to move at short notice. At which point your negotiating position will be weak and you will end up paying a premium.

Do your homework – Don't believe what you are told - You may well be getting mugged.

So the advice would be, when you have a break clause or rent review coming up, be prepared to move. Give the necessary notice, via your lawyers, so there is a record of the notice. Find alternative premises and let it be known that you have. Make preparations to leave, and see what your landlord comes back with. His game will be to leave it till the last minute by not returning your calls, push you into a corner where you have nowhere else to go, then hike up the rent. You pay the inflated price because you now have no choice. This sets a new high to what is referred to as the *Fair Market Price*, and everybody's business rates increase accordingly. Businesses go bust, the Charity shops move in, and we have another employment blackspot. You owe it to yourself and the community to get this right.

Can I trust my surveyor?

As we have discussed, many surveyors work for the landlord, and can mislead you into paying a higher rent. That way the landlord will give them more business.

Some surveyors will pick on the highest rents paid and try to convince you there is a real shortage of commercial property around so you will pay even higher rent. It is this greed that, as we have said, results in charity shops all over our high streets, the loss of jobs and the destruction of our local communities. It is wrong and needs exposing.

We have looked at conflicts of interests, but it gets worse, within *Ratings Surveyors* there are those who deal exclusively with *Rates Appeals*. If you are asked for money up front, be careful. Find out what their success rate is. The good guys are getting 30%+ the bad guys are just processing the paperwork and get very low, say 5%, success rate. The contract you sign can exclude you from running another appeal so you get stuck with the cost of the appeal and high rates for the duration of the contract.

Having said that there are some very good ratings surveyors out there who will know the availability of your type of property in an area and can advise you where to look. They will be able to supply a range of rents currently being paid. They can do this because that is how they undertake the rates appeals. They will put you in a position of choice and, if you like, handle the negotiation for you.

Find the right Surveyor – Agree a fee for the job in advance.

What about business rates?

Business rates are a real bug bear of mine. They should be abolished for the trouble and cost they cause business. They are a tax on innovation and entrepreneurship. They are also a gift to bureaucratic job creation schemes, another tax on innovation and real jobs that pay for themselves.

The first thing you need to know about business rates is that they are a matter of Public Record and they are available from the Valuation Office. Phone your local office and ask them. In my experience, unlike some Councils officers, the Valuation Office know what they are doing and can be very helpful.

Business rates have historically been 40% of rents. They are a significant chunk of your premises costs. Recently with the drop in rents this percentage has increased. I had a 20,000 square foot warehouse where we were able to renegotiate the rent downwards, leaving the rates at 120% of the rent. Not funny.

Think about small business rate relief. If you can get a smaller part of a larger building and go for a separate assessment. This can, under current legislation, result in no rates being payable at all.

Know what you are going to pay up front - Check it is right - Don't believe what you are told.

What are dilapidations?

Dilapidations are something to be very wary of. When you sign a lease you take on some responsibility for the repair of the building. Make sure you have representative photographs of all the building actually attached to and part of your lease document. Otherwise at the end of your lease your landlord can present you with a bill to repair his building to its original state. This is a very real threat. I know of many people who have fallen foul of this pitfall. You think it is a level playing field – It is not.

Always be careful about Dilapidations.

Consult a Lawyer.

Should I sign a personal guarantee?

Do not sign a personal guarantee if you can possibly avoid it. Always sign the lease in the name of a limited company, never give cross guarantees. I have seen many people become badly unstuck by unscrupulous (The Polite Word) landlords. If you cannot get a deal without a personal guarantee I would seriously question whether you should take on the property.

Not if you can help it.

> ### *A Cautionary Tale*
>
> I know of a business who acquired a subsidiary company into which to place business it was subcontracting. During the negotiations the lease ran out, and the Directors of the new company were put under pressure by the landlord to provide a cross guarantee from the holding company. This they did when they became Directors of the acquiring group. The extra work supplied to the new company meant that the building soon became too small. It was time to move. However despite the holding company finding perfectly suitable tenants for the building, the landlord preferred the security of the guarantee from the holding company. They ended up with a new building and paying £60k pa for three years until the end of the leases. Cost £180,000. In those days empty properties did not attract business rates. Now they do.

Do not give Directors of acquired companies a place on the Group Board, or the ability to sign anything, until you know them better.

Should I use a lawyer?

Always use a lawyer, and again ask around, find out who has a good commercial property department and a good Partner. You want someone who will help the deal go through. Some lawyers run up their bills and make the situation worse. This is not about winning it is about negotiating flexibility in case you need it. The right surveyor might also be able to steer you in the right direction here. No harm in having more than one lawyer.

If your lawyer advises you that your lease is unusually onerous this might well be a sign that the landlord has every intention of enforcing the clauses. They are there for a reason. Walk away. This is why you need to have more than one option in the first place. That way you will find the best compromise for your business.

Always use a lawyer – This is not a level playing field.

Property people are often bullies – You need protection.

A Success Story

There are good landlords out there, again especially ones that share your vision.

British Airports Authority BAA, were both our Landlords and our clients, we were doing a good job for them, and as we came out of the 1990's recession we were hit with a bad debt, and fell behind with the rent.

We approached BAA and offered to secure the outstanding rent by offering them a *Debenture,* their position was secured, and we received a sizeable loan at a rate we could not have achieved elsewhere.

For the record - Thank you BAA.

What about working from home?

Lots of people work from home, it is the most cost effective option, the attraction is cost, the downside is lack of privacy, being interrupted, and not being able to leave your work at work. A good place to start but you cannot really build a team at home. What about Virtual teams? Well yes, it depends upon the sector and the level of experience and discipline. Be wary of becoming a consultant forever. How are you going to scale your business from home? Think it through, what are the income streams, where are the *Dripping Roasts?*

Serviced offices and hubs

There is a great deal to be said for incubator offices with a range of skills all with low overheads and as such can be very cost effective.

There is a real danger however of starting to think like small company people. Be wary of who you spend your time with.

There are specialist Incubator units such as Stevenage Bio Science Catalyst, and St John's Innovation centre that have developed as centres of excellence.

Look for an incubator hub with the right mix of skills and a sharing culture.

Sources of help

Andrew Bacon   JMA Chartered Surveyors - http://www.jmacs.co.uk

Longmores Solicitors Commercial Property - http://www.longmores -solicitors.co.uk/site/services_business/commercial_property/

Visit http://www.welhatchamber.co.uk/thrive-and-survive to access a continually updated web page of useful links.

Further reading

Commercial Lease Bible – *Jean Louis Racine*

Chapter 5 - Cash Flow and Gross Profit

"Look at that Johnstone, we are flying along
- What do you mean I cannot buy a new car??"

"Happiness is a positive cash flow" Fred Adler

*"The fact is that one of the earliest lessons I learned in business
was that balance sheets and income statements are fiction,
cash flow is reality"* Chris Chocola

Cash is King. You really do need to know what is going on with cash.
However, that is easily said. Cash is the last stage of the sales process,
what comes before is where we need to look.

Businesses fail because they run out of cash. Well ultimately yes, but
they run out of time to do something about it first.

The Waterwheel Model

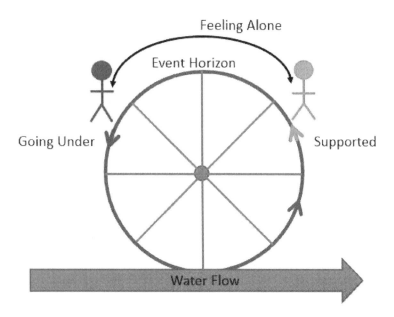

Each growth stage of your business is fraught with uncertainty and risk. You can get it right 20 times in a row but you only have to get it wrong once to lose your business. Always remember that :-

The WHY controls your gross profit, the amount that each sale contributes to your overhead, your cash flow. A £1000 sale at 60% GP contributes £600, at 10% GP only £100.

The WHAT is the product mix, the range of products into different markets at different GP%'s. It is this mix that controls your cash flow today.

The HOW is the learning organisation that delivers your next source of high margin products into new markets and hence your future cash flow and the sustainability of your business.

Questions

1. What is Cash Flow?
2. Where does your cash flow come from?
3. Do you know what your cash flow, debtors and creditors position will be next month?
4. How are you tracking the changing gross profit of each product over time?
5. Every product or service has a shelf life. What are your plans to address this?
6. Should you sell the low GP parts of the business?
7. Where will the next cash generating product come from?
8. If margins in current markets are declining, are there new markets available to you?
9. Where will you find help?

Think About

What is cash flow?

Cash flow is the balance between the cash coming into your business and the timings of the payments you make out of your business. When people talk about cash flow projections they mean a view of your future sales at a given *gross profit* contributing to your overhead as discussed in Chapter 2, but then taking account of the timings of payments. If your customers pay you on 60 days and you pay your suppliers on 30 days, then you will have to find the cash to fund 30 days' worth of payments for staff costs, overheads and materials suppliers.

So it is important to manage your cash properly, especially in a small business.

If you can part invoice up front you should do so. You should invoice as promptly as you can. If you can date the invoices for the month in which the work was done. An invoice Due on 30 days dated the 31st August will probably be paid in September. An Invoice date the 1st September may well be paid in October. So if you turn over £100,000 a month this could make 100,000 plus Vat = £120,000 difference to your cash flow for October.

Cash incidentally refers to the cash you have in your bank account(s).

Always remember
CASH IS KING!!!

Where does your cash flow come from?

Ultimately your cash flow comes from your brand. Your customers' perception of the value they gain as a result of their relationship with your business.

Every time you do a quote, you put this to the test. Effectively you are testing the *Price Elasticity* of the market. How much are your customers prepared to pay before they switch to a cheaper source?

If they believe in your brand, they will be loyal and pay a premium to support you. If not, you are competing on price.

It is VITAL that you know where you are on this. So you must know how much gross profit you are making on each quote and how much you give away if you compromise on price.

The extent of the pressure to compromise on price will depend upon your cash flow forecast for the coming months. If you need the sales compromise, if not don't. I come back to the motor cycle analogy, you need to know the line round the bend, when to accelerate and when to brake. That line is your gross profit%.

The road to misery lies in not understanding your cash flow –

That is YOU – not your accountant

Do you know your next month's cash flow?

You need to have a decent Profit & Loss **(P&L)** and cash flow model running in your business. In our increasingly fast changing world, it is not enough to be told how you are doing yearly, quarterly or monthly in arrears. You need to know your bank, debtors and creditors positions, in advance based upon your order book and outstanding quotes.

If this is uncertain then take back control of expenditure, and reduce outgoings.

This is how you know that you understand your cash flow

How are you tracking the changing gross profit?

We have looked at measuring GP on a quote by quote, sale by sale basis, but we need to understand what is happening in the minds of our customers. Are our products becoming less fashionable, yesterday's story? If so, we will spot this in the falling GP of that product group. So we need to be monitoring GP by individual sale and by product group to know where we are.

This is how you track the life-stage of each of your products.

It is how you know when you need to find new products.

> ### A Cautionary Tale
>
> I know of a family business who had been in business for three generations. As the world changed they bought the building and invested in new machinery. The new machinery bought new clients and new work opportunities. They took on a contract for some £250k, but had not worked out the margins. Some three month later they were short of £100k of cash flow. They were so concerned they pretty much decided to shut the business. What had happened was that they were accustomed to making 50% GP ie £125k but in this case they were only making 10% GP, that is £25k and that is where the £100k had gone.

> ### Always measure your GP% at the Quote Stage.

Every product or service has a shelf life. What are your plans to address this?

The point being that as GP%'s drop so do your profits and cash flow. Over time this makes you vulnerable to take over, or just becoming irrelevant to your customers' needs. See the *Waterwheel Model*.

This why you must find the new products.

> **Remember to monitor your Gross Profit by Product range.**
>
> **Learn how to reinvent yourself and create new products.**

Should you sell the low GP parts of the business?

Well this is a big point, and it has to do with *Change Management*. It is a mistake I have made personally. Sometimes your staff are so loyal to a product range and have believed in that product for so long, that to tell them to drop it, and start believing in some uncertain future, can be difficult.

As David Gill of St John's Innovation Centre Cambridge said to me

> *"Nick - People don't like to kill their Children".*

He is right of course, sometimes you can run with loyalty to staff, and not wanting to disrupt a successful team. The problem being that as the margins fall, pure economics will disrupt the team anyway. Sometimes you should sell the business, or part of the business, and let those staff do what they are best at in new markets.

Sometimes it is better to sell teams and customers, rather than reinvent them.

Where will the next cash generating product come from?

OK at this point we start to move from the conceptual and understanding part of this section into a more analytical phase. Your next cash generating product will come from the minds of your staff and customers. At this stage we will simply introduce the concepts of selling products into five different types of markets. From a cash flow perspective each market will progressively require a greater amount of cash flow before they deliver a return on investment.

Those five markets types are:-

1. ***Outsmarting the Competition*** - What existing customers want now.
2. ***Customer Led Incremental*** - Continuously improving existing products to existing customers.
3. ***Customer Led New Markets*** - Continuously improving existing products to new customers.
4. ***Step Change - New Markets*** - Existing products to different market new country and culture.
5. ***Step Change - New Products*** - Cross-selling new products to new and existing Customers.

Think about this, then see   ***Chapter 6 - Marketing and Chapter 9 – Innovation***

If margins in current markets are declining, are there new markets available to you?

Innovation Adoption

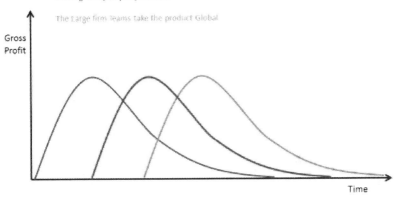

The Micro / Small teams come up with a new idea, this is taken up by the Early Adopters

The Small / Medium teams move that product into new Early Adopter markets and existing Early Majority markets

The Large firm Teams take the product Global

The GP on nearly all products declines over time as competition joins the market or they are simply not new anymore.

> **When your existing products are starting to feel old in your current markets, it's time to find new markets.**

It is worth considering this, in terms of how customers adopt innovation.

Customer Adoption Phases

Innovation Adoption Lifecycle

Early Adopters are the enquiring minds, they are forgiving, it is not that important if the product does not work properly. They want to know how it works and be associated with its newness. These people are happy to pay a premium for newness.

Early Majority are generally well off, like newness but look for some reliability. They want it new but they want it to work. Perhaps they take themselves a little seriously, they want the Geeks to take the risks but not be seen to be out of touch.

Late Majority these folk are less well off, but don't want to be seen to be left behind. They want to get what the Early Majority got, but 20% cheaper.

Laggards these folk only buy digital phones because you cannot get analogue any more.

Think about the maturity of your current markets, are you selling established products into a mature market? Are your customers predominantly in the early and late majority stages? Are your margins just starting to slide?

Know where you are today

Think about the five market types that are available to you. We will start to quantify the cash flow implications of moves into these markets in **Chapter 9 - Innovation**

Understand the Time, Skills and Cash implications of moving into a new market

> *Understand the relationship between your gross profit and the adoption phases in each new market.*

Sources of help

Penny Barr   Barr Associates - http://www.barrandassociates.com/

Mark Novitt   Novitt Harris - http://www.novittharris.com/

Norman Cowan   Wilder Coe - http://www.wildercoe.co.uk/

http://www.welhatchamber.co.uk/thrive-and-survive

Further reading

Rich Dad Poor Dad: What The Rich Teach Their Kids About Money - That The Poor and Middle Class Do Not! - *Robert T. Kiyosaki*

Chapter 6 – Marketing

"Ultimately the value of a brand resides in the mind of the customer" David Ogilvy

"It is not about doing "Digital Marketing", it is about marketing effectively in a digital world" Ivan Menzes

The key thing to understand about marketing is that customers take decisions with the *"Emotional"* side of their brain, then use the *"Rational"* side of their brain to justify the decision.

Either they want it, or they don't.

The price they are happy to pay is dependent upon how much they want it.

So the real question is - How do you ensure that people want a relationship with your business?

Marketing engages with your customers to build a relationship with them so when they decide to make a purchase they choose to purchase your product, over that of your competitors' products, because they want to, and because they understand the reputation of your product so they are not too concerned about the price.

The WHY - The belief in *The Force for Good* - the *Emotional Differentiator* "I want that handbag because I believe in Hermes"

The WHAT - The range of fashionable products, the convenience, the customer experience and the product quality. The *Rational Differentiators* that help to justify the prices in today's markets.

The HOW - The evolving knowledge and understanding of the changing customer needs that will deliver The WHAT in tomorrow's markets.

Questions

1. How do you differentiate your business from your competition?
2. What are the Brand Promises you make?
3. Which of those are Emotional, which are Rational?
4. Which are Aspirational, which are to be expected? A Given?
5. How do you manage your relationship with existing customers?
6. Do you have a view as to which customers are Detractors, Passives or Advocates of your products?
7. How do you manage Customer Experience?
8. What stories would you like your customers to tell about their relationship with your brand?
9. How do you measure this?

Think About

The job of marketeers is to ensure that your organisation is a survivor. They do that by ensuring that customers want your organisation's products because they make them feel good about themselves, and hence are happy to pay a premium for those products.

How do you differentiate your business?

If your business looks and feels the same as the next, why should a customer pay extra for your products? If this is the case, you compete on price and this is a game of diminishing returns leading to oblivion.

So it is important to know WHY your business exists. WHY you are a *"Force for Good"*. So that you, your staff and your customers can believe in what you are doing.

The WHY - *The Forces for Good are the Emotional Differentiators*.

Customers and staff want to believe in and be part of that better world, and so are prepared to give more to your organisation, be that time, skills, recommendations or cash.

The *Rational Differentiators* are the WHAT and the HOW. What you do and how you do it are the proof that you believe in the WHY.

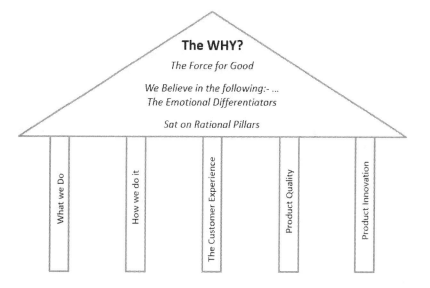

If you look and feel the same as everyone else – How will your customers find you?

What are your *Brand Promises*?

It is probably easiest to demonstrate this with a live example, with a broad client base, so taking the Chamber of Commerce, for example:-

Welwyn Hatfield
Chamber of Commerce

Understanding and Delivering our Members' Goals

We promise to Understand and Deliver our Members' Goals

We believe that:-

- Our members are important. What they do, matters to all of us.
- Our members should be supported and not feel alone.
- We should minimise risk to business owners wherever possible.
- We should look after the families and staff of business owners wherever possible.
- We should provide good information to help inform better decisions & reduce stress.
- We should help member businesses grow.
- We should provide access to skills and working capital.

Trust is built by delivering against written and unwritten promises.

Which of these differentiators are *Emotional*, which are *Rational*?

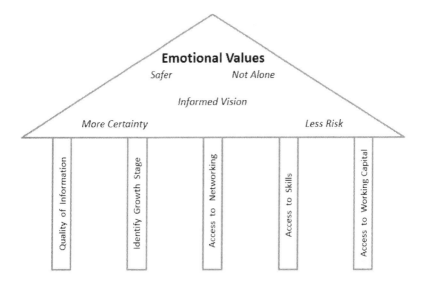

> **Breach a rational promise and disappoint -**
>
> **Breach an emotional one and make an enemy.**

Which are *Aspirational*, which are to be expected? *A Given*?

Here we are putting ourselves in the mind of the customer. We think that our members aspire to:--

1.   Drive the vision of their business.
2.   Do this as part of a supportive community.
3.   Minimise risk for their staff and families.
4.   Attract the best customers.

We would hope that our members can trust and expect a high standard from our:-

1.   Quality of Information.
2.   Understanding of their current business Growth Stages.
3.   Networking events.
4.   Recommendations re Skills Sourcing.
5.   Recommendations re Working Capital Sourcing.

Disappoint on expectations and spoil today, disappoint on aspirations and spoil tomorrow

How do you manage your relationship with existing customers?

1.   We attend a number of events.
2.   We look to join up resource to better serve our customers.
3.   We run monthly newsletters to communicate our activities.
4.   We try to engage with our members at all opportunities.
5.   We invite members to join our e-Publishing Group and contribute to events.
6.   We look to build relationships with community influencers.
7.   We are seen to stand up for the interests of our members.
8.   We promote debate in social media.

*By Listening, Understanding, and Improving –
It is an Iterative process.*

Which customers are *Detractors, Passives or Promoters*?

Do you know which are which? Well, yes we do, from a number of sources, but we should practice what we preach and do more.

Net Promoter scores are ideal for this because they ask two very simple questions.

Question 1. How likely are you to recommend our products and services to your contacts and colleagues?

Score 0 to 10 -
0 not likely
10 very likely

Scores of   0,1,2,3 –   Detractors
                4,5,6 -   Passives
                7,8,9,10 – Promoters

Based upon a simple count take your detractors and passives from your promoters to give a number, your net promoter score. These can then be compared with each other.

Question 2.

The promoters are then asked a secondary question:

"What is the one thing we are getting right that you would like to see more of?"

Passives and detractors are asked:

"What is the one thing we are not getting right that you would like to see improved?"

This enables the CEO to act upon under-performing areas of his business and identify an action plan.

He writes personally to the customer base, collects the responses, speaks to the brand manager, tells him what needs fixing and then, repeats the question in three months' time.

How do you manage *Customer Experience*?

Personally - We said at the start of this chapter that marketing is about managing *Customer Expectations*.

The Three Phases of Communication

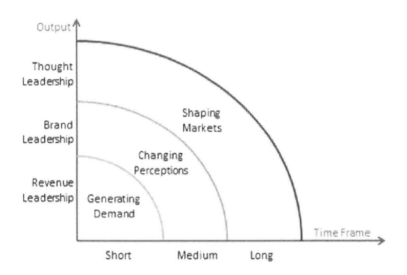

There are Three Phases to this:

1. Short *Term*   -   **The WHAT** - Get some sales in to generate cash to build your brand.
2. *Medium Term* - **The HOW** - Build trust with your customers. Become "The Guardian of their Aspirations".
   Help them to become trusted and respected by their peers.
   Change perceptions through the Early Adopters.
3. *Long Term*   -   **The WHY** - Build on that trust to Shape Markets, through thought leadership.

Expectation Management

So far we have looked at *External Communications* - our brand promise to deliver the things we believe in. Having created that expectation, the customer experience had better exceed that expectation. That is, your staff had better believe as well. Internal communications will be dealt with in more detail in *Change Management* in **Chapter 7 - Team Building**.

Customer experience interfaces with all levels of your business, and it evolves daily – Monitor it.

A Cautionary Tale

A major international clothing retailer, looked to engage with their customers by involving them in a competition to rebrand their stores. An impressive 2% of their loyal customer base responded and in due course, across the world, their stores adverts websites stationery and all their communications collateral were converted to the new branding. The problem was that the 98% who had not been consulted hated it and there was such a fuss that the store had to revert to their original branding.

Had the retailer just rebranded, it would have been fine. What happened was that unintentionally they engaged with 2% of their customer base, of which there was only one winner, and effectively excluded the 98%. The Emotional reaction was significant.

Which stories would you like your customers to tell about you?

I would like our members to tell their colleagues about how their business has thrived in part as a result of the support from the Chamber.

Seek testimonials - Invite constructive criticism - Monitor social media

How do you measure this?

1. Attendance at events.
2. Website Google Stats.
3. Newsletter Open Rates.
4. Membership numbers.
5. Return on Investment (ROI) on Marketing Activity.
6. We could use products such as Radian 6 to monitor Social Media.
7. We are considering running customer engagement tools such as Marketo.

Marketing is about managing expectations. It should set the scene, make the customer feel comfortable with your values and help him feel somehow better about him or herself as a result of their relationship with your brand.

So you need to decide which of your products and services make **Who** feel good about themselves and **Why**. That is - Which *Products* are you selling into which *Target Markets* and how are you different from the competition in a good way? – *Your Differentiators.*

It's that diagram again. Be clear about which products sell to whom and why.

The Product GP Lifecycle

Each product has its time, its "Must Have" moment, when the *Early Adopters* and *Early Majority* are buying.

Supply and Demand dictates that new players will come into the market, compete on price and, over time, reduce the margins

Gross Profit

Time

Now within each target market there is a range of behaviour.

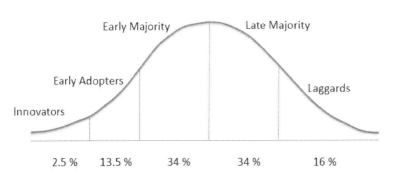

Customer Adoption Phases

| Innovators | Early Adopters | Early Majority | Late Majority | Laggards |
| 2.5 % | 13.5 % | 34 % | 34 % | 16 % |

Innovation Adoption Lifecycle

Innovators and *Early Adopters* will support you because they believe in what you do. They will pay a premium to be ahead of the trend curve. They feel good about themselves because they are informed and able to help. They are also forgiving about teething problems because they like to help. So this is high margin business, but it is only 15% of the market.

Marketeers talk about *"Crossing the Gap"* that is the gap between the *Early Adopters* and the *Early Majority*. The *Early Majority* are one third of the market, and where they go the *Late Majority* will follow as will the *Laggards* eventually. The Gap is that the *Early Adopters* do not make good reference sites for the more cautious *Early Majority*. The Early Majority will wait for *other Early Majority* adopters to adopt, so there is a gap. (This gap is illustrated on the front cover.)

The *Early Majority* will only engage once they have seen the *Early Adopters* go through the teething problems. They feel good about themselves because they did not take that risk, typically they will get a small discount on the initial price, so they will feel wise as well. They are the *Early Majority* because they have a need to keep up with the *Fashion*. They don't want the risk but they don't want to be out of date either. So this is where the money is, *High Volume* and *High Margin* sales.

At this point the market changes, the *Early Adopters* move on to the next innovative opportunity, and the *Late Majority* join the fray. These people are less concerned about fashion and trends, they will wait for a year and buy last year's model at a reduced price.

At this point you are in a *High Volume* but increasingly *Low Margin* market. We look at this further in **Chapter 8 - Innovation**. Remember what is old hat in existing markets can be new elsewhere.

Product Lifecycle:- Sales and Profits

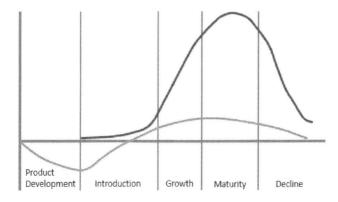

It is worth mentioning that these concepts hold true from accountancy services to plumbing. In every group of people there is a cross section of propensity to take risk. We all want value for money, but the price we are prepared to pay for status or recognition varies widely and depends upon a range of factors from wealth to education to life stage to location to your genetic makeup.

One key learning piece here is that marketing drives fashion. Once you are ahead of the curve, and are driving opinion and preferences then your customers will self-select their behaviour. All you need is the ability to define and structure your market and quantify your *Return on Investment* ROI -That is - each time you crank the marketing handle it costs X and generates X+++.

7 things to remember in marketing:

1. Manage Communications across your organisation.
2. Informed by a Customer Mind-set.
3. Guided by Customer Insight.
4. Co-Create Value with your Customers.
5. The Innovative and Iterative process.
6. Organise around your Customers.
7. Test, Measure, Learn, Repeat.

I cannot finish off a chapter on marketing without mentioning Social Media more fully. This is clearly a subject worthy of its own book, but to get social right it is even more important that you understand the drivers of human behaviour. The point about social is that the brands have lost their monopoly of the media, your staff and customers both have their own media now – the internet in all its forms. This is why *Customer Experience* and the belief in the *Force for Good* are coming to the fore. This sounds like accountability to me and long may it last.

My mentor Gary Hamel in his excellent book **What Matters Now**, says that

> *"Successful organisations of the future will,*
>
> *Align the Values of their Brand their Customers and their Staff"*

This concept should be central to your thinking. Consider it a *Mantra* for success.

ALSO

> *"It is not about doing 'Digital Marketing', It is about marketing effectively in a Digital World."*

Sources of help

Welwyn Hatfield Chamber of Commerce -
http://www.welhatchamber.co.uk/
nick@welhatchamber.co.uk

Steve Harris, Cartoonist and Illustrator -
http://www.steveharrisillustration.com
info@steveharrisillustration.co.uk

Simon Sinek Ted Talk - https://www.ted.com/talks/simon_sinek_
how_great_leaders_inspire_action?language=en

Visit http://www.welhatchamber.co.uk/thrive-and-survive to access
a continually updated web page of useful links.

Further reading

What Matters Now - *Gary Hamel.*

Brilliant Social Media: How to start, refine and improve your social
business media strategy - *Adam Gray*

Chapter 7 - Raising Finance

"A bank is a place that will lend you money if you can prove that you don't need it." Bob Hope

The reason that **Raising Finance** comes in at Chapter 7, is that I don't think that you should borrow money before you have understood, and your business has reached the growth stages covered by the contents of Chapters 1 to 6. That is to say that:-

1. You have a plan.
2. That is delivering cash-paying customers.
3. Looked after by the right team of people.
4. From the right premises.
5. So you have established your sales and gross profit contribution to your overhead, allowing you to know which products are producing how much surplus cash.

That surplus cash is now paying for the marketing that is generating a known return of additional cash flow. Every time you crank the marketing handle it generates X amount of surplus cash.

You now want to scale your business to pursue market share before your competitors catch up.

The thing about borrowing money is that you have to pay it back. I see lots of people borrowing money because someone says they need *Working Capital* to start a business.

I say NO!! – You need customers and positive cash flow to start a business; without these you will end up worse off, with no business, and debts to repay with no way to repay them.

So generate cash first so you can repay the loans. There are times when borrowing money is the right thing to do. As we have discussed, periodically you will need to reinvent yourself or your products. All change carries risks, the trick is to quantify those risks, so you choose the low risk high upside options.

We will explore this now, basically before borrowing money you should be very clear about the answers to following questions.

Questions

Do you know:-

1. What do you want the money for?
2. How much will you need?
3. How long will you need it for?
4. What is the potential upside?
5. If it does not work out how will you repay the interest and capital borrowed?
6. What security are you being asked for?
7. If you looking for *Debt Finance* - that is loan or overdraft. What is the APR?
8. What is APR?
9. What about *Asset Finance* – that is a loan secured against a car or debtors or a piece of machinery?
10. What about an *Equity Partner*, active or passive?
11. When should you use a *Venture Capitalist*?
12. Which grants are available and how do you source them?
13. What are your chances of obtaining a grant?
14. About Crowdsourcing?

Think About

As you can see this is a complex area. The number you need to nail is how much free cash is your business generating. Then decide if you are prepared to risk that on your next expansion plan. Be clear about how you quantify that risk. See **Chapter 9 - Innovation**.

What do you want the money for?

You should be clear that you should only borrow money to help you expand your business. Do not borrow money because someone tells you need working capital. What you need is a business that generates cash from day one.

If your business is not generating cash how are you going to repay the Loan?

So be clear about how this extra working capital is going to help you build your business.

> *If you don't know what the money is for -*
>
> *How will you know it is generating the cash to repay the loan?*

How much will you need?

This is a classic example of where you might need some help. Try to find someone who is financially literate, but who also has the business experience of taking the step you are considering. They will know what it will cost to break into a new market. Crunch the numbers, see how much your existing cash flow will help finance your working capital requirement. Think about how confident you are in the numbers. Have you tested the market? Do you know that if you are spending £1000 and it is consistently returning £1200, that if you spent £10,000 it would return £12,000 or more? Does the concept scale? Test and repeat.

Seriously consider running a *Joint Venture* with someone already operating in that market, let them take the risk and share in the profits. Always manage downside risk. Your hard earned cash and assets are at stake.

You are not alone

Don't borrow more than you need.

If you are fooling yourself that things will get better, and are borrowing money to maintain a lifestyle, don't do it. Cut back and wait until things have got better.

If you cannot quantify the cash flow risk – Why take the risk?

How long will you need it for?

If you do borrow money and there is uncertainty, subject to reasonable interest rates, try to borrow over a longer period than you need, and check that there are no early repayment penalties.

That way you will have built some options and flexibility into the exercise.

Buy Flexibility in the timing – you might be grateful you did

What is the potential upside?

If it works, how will you demonstrate that so you can scale the opportunity before every one jumps on the band wagon?

Scale operations when the time is right - Carpe Diem - Seize the Day.

How will you repay the interest and capital borrowed?

If the answer is that this is coming from your personal reserves, do not do it. If the answer is that it will come from existing business cash flow, then assess the upside and downside risks and take a view. - *Be sure of the downside risk.*

What security are you being asked for?

If you are asked for a personal guarantee, be very careful. You are committing your reserves, but also you put yourself at the mercy of unscrupulous people. What happens if they withdraw other sources of funding, so you run out of cash? They would not do that I hear you say! Well they do, and do so frequently. The banks make more money when you default. So be very careful.

There is a concept called *Boiled Frog Syndrome* the theory is that if you drop a frog into hot water it will jump out sharpish, but if you put him in cold water and bring it to the boil, he will sit there and cook. I have certainly continued to put money and time into a business, not realised how hot the water was getting, and should have jumped out earlier. I think that you just don't want to admit defeat. At least that is how it feels. If the market has moved on, sometimes there is nothing you can do about it. That is not defeat it is simply reality.

Your existing assets are hard earned – Don't put them at risk - Easily said

If you are looking for *Debt Finance* - What is the APR?

Do you know the difference between a Loan and an Overdraft? Well an overdraft is designed to tide you over short term cash flow issues; a bad debt for example. It may be recalled at any time, and your bank manager will expect an overdraft to be being slowly repaid over time. Companies that are up against their overdraft limit are considered to be a bad risk, and pay higher rates of interest accordingly. The APR is the Annualised Percentage rate. It is the real interest rate you pay on a reducing loan.

Understand the banks expectations and what it will cost you

A Worked example on APR

OK this is a useful concept to understand to ensure that you are comparing like with like. When you are comparing, a rental agreement to a lease to HP or to an overdraft to pay cash. It is probably best explained with a worked example.

If you borrow £100,000 over 10 months at a flat interest rate of 10%. Then the total interest is £10,000. So each month you pay back £10,000 capital and £1000 interest. All very straight forward you might think. Except it's not. Because at the end of Month One you are only borrowing £90,000 and yet you still pay £1000 in interest. So over the course of the loan you are only borrowing an average of Half the £100,000 = £50,000, and yet you are paying £10,000 in interest so the true interest rate is 20%. In fact when you do the flat rate calculation for your accounting purposes, this is the calculation you do. The APR however is normally the flat rate times 2 plus 1% so in this case 21%. This is because the bank will normally allocate interest against the capital to reduce the outstanding balance quicker in the early months. This reduces their tax bill on interest receivable, and improves their stress testing ratios.

Understand Basic Financial terms and how they affect you

What about *Asset Finance*?

Asset Finance is a loan secured against a car or debtors or a piece of machinery?

Hunt around. Enquire from other business people. There are some real rogues in this business.

A Cautionary Tale

Back in the 90's we took out a lease agreement on a £20k printer to undertake high volume black and white print very cost effectively. As it turned out the machine did not do what it said on the tin. It took a few thousand copies to warm up and we had the maintenance engineers out all the time resulting in our nearly missing client deadlines and being up half the night too many times. So we recognised that flexibility and no single point of failure was better, even if the pence per copy was higher, and bought 10 smaller machines. Some of which are still working today. We agreed with the engineers that the machine was consistently not performing to specification, and sent it back. About a week later I got a very concerned call from the director of the business who had signed the paperwork. She had just had a visit, at her home address, from two gentleman saying that she had signed a personal guarantee and was liable for the capital plus outstanding interest over the term of the agreement amounting to some £30k, and could she sign the paperwork they brought with them. You can imagine that did not go down well. Fortunately she did not sign anything and I was able to reassure her that we had been asked for a personal guarantee, but that I had refused to give it, and that the paperwork she had signed did not create any personal liability. It still did not stop them trying it on.

Read the small print, starting with the last clause. The bad clauses are normally near the end.

Always read documents before you sign them – especially financial documents

If there is a clause where you **indemnify** the lender, don't sign it. Or strike out the Indemnity Clause. Giving an indemnity allows the other party to sue you and you agree to pay their legal costs. So taking the printer story above, these guys could have supplied a not fit for purpose machine, then sued you, and you would have had to pay all their legal costs which they would string out, and hold you over a barrel.

"I'm here about the details."

What about an *Equity Partner*?

One way to raise money and gain skills is to sell some shares in your business and take on an equity partner. If you can find the right person with the investment capital, the right experience and contacts, this can be very valuable. 75% of something is better than 100% of nothing.

Many *Equity Partners* say they do not want to be involved, but then interfere and can be a problem.

My advice would be find someone who is either properly involved, so you can grow together, or not Involved at all in the day to day running of the business.

> ***Be clear whether you are looking for cash, skills or both.***
>
> ***Define the skills carefully.***

When you should you use a *Venture Capitalist*?

The short answer is "When you want someone else to run your business".

The basic facts are that something like one in ten investments pay out for the venture capitalists, so when they do pay out they have to cover the costs of the failures and then some. It is also true that they are ten times more likely to get a result when they employ a professional manager in to run the business instead of the founder.

So the chances of you continuing to run your business are small.

Speak to owners of other businesses they have invested in – Good and Bad

Which grants are available and how do you source them?

Grants are an interesting subject. It seems that you need an inside track to get grants. 94% of people who applied for European Grants in Hertfordshire wasted their time last year – that is a lot of time.

However certain consultants claim to have a 100% success rate. How can this be?

Well it is not about the project, it is about making your project fit the *Funding Criteria*, and knowing how to fill in the forms.

The other issue is that there are a number of time consuming compliance criteria which you have to report on. This really is an area for specialist knowledge.

Find the right advisor with a track record in your sector. Speak to satisfied clients

What are your chances of obtaining a grant?

Depends on your contacts and the project. Generally, very slim.

Find the right advisor

What about Crowdsourcing?

On the face of it *Crowdsourcing* offers lots of opportunities. Lots of people investing money they can afford to lose because they believe in what you are doing.

The main barrier here is having the skills to get your message out to lots of people and have some investors lined up before the launch. Crowd funding is well-named - investors follow the Crowd.

If you start with a slow burn you are unlikely to attract investors.

Get your PR right

Sources of help

Julian Chapman   Leopardrockcapital
http://www.leopardrockcapital.com/

Visit http://www.welhatchamber.co.uk/thrive-and-survive to access a continually updated web page of useful links.

Further reading

The Finance and Funding Directory 2014/15: A comprehensive guide to the best sources of finance and funding – *Jonathan Wooler*

Chapter 8 - Team Building

"Pete, Barry go to the garden centre and get some lime. Sarah and George go to the paint shop and get some dust sheets. Nick check out Google Maps and find some quiet woodland nearby. The rest of you can help me bury the facilitator. Who ironically has just led the most highly motivated team building exercise we have ever had."

"Successful people build each other up. They motivate, inspire and push each other."

"What sets apart high-performance teams is how committed the members are to each other." Katzenbach & Smith

"Management is doing things right; leadership is doing the right things." Peter F Drucker

Joking apart, team building is the most important part of your business.

The WHY is the shared vision that will hold your teams together, and make them trust each other.

The WHAT is what your teams are accountable for delivering to your customers today.

The HOW is your ideas and innovation nursery, it is how your teams work together, sharing and transferring knowledge, so the best people can advance. It is the learning organisation. It is how your teams know that they are the best in their field. The HOW is the Engine Room for innovation and the future of your business.

Do not forget that you are a key member of the team, your role is to fill your management team with all the necessary confidence and skills to deliver against your dream. Non-Exec Directors can be very useful here. There is plenty of evidence that suggests that successful businesses start out with the right depth and breadth of skills on their board from the very beginning.

Make sure - You are not alone

Questions

1. Who should you have on your top management team?
2. Should you grow your business?
3. How does employing more staff cause problems?
4. How should you build teams of people? *Delegation vs Abrogation.*
5. How do you build confidence in your teams?
6. Who should you have in each team?
7. How should you reward your best people?
8. How do you build successful teams?
9. Having built your first teams - What happens next?
10. What about the review process?
11. Managing people is difficult, what are the guiding lights?

Think About

When it comes to building teams there are two types, the top management team, and then the teams that run the day to day business.

The top team runs the **WHY** and manages the **WHAT** and the **HOW**.

The other teams run the **WHAT** and the **HOW.**

Let's look at the characteristics of the top team first.

Who should you have on your top management team?

1. You should have diverse and flexible skills.
2. You should not build clones of yourself and a self-appreciation society.
3. You should have people who will challenge and support you.
4. People whose skills are complimentary.

Try to avoid this.

Bill Gross of IdeasLab recently identified two consistent differentiators between successful and unsuccessful businesses. The first was being in the right place at the right time, the second was having a broad range of skills amongst the founding partners and their advisors.

So you will need someone to:-

1. See the opportunity and plan the business.
2. Bring the sales in.
3. Produce the goods and manage the staff.
4. Find the right premises and do the legal stuff.
5. Add up the profits.
6. Understand the customers changing needs.
7. Raise capital to scale the business.
8. Build the teams with the skills to scale the business.
9. Know when the business needs to reinvent itself.
10. Find new markets for existing and evolving products.
11. Know when the time is right to sell, and manage that for you.
12. Understand how communities are developing around your activities.

This does not mean a team of 12, you may well be able to cover most of them yourself, but you should have a few people up to 5, who not only cover these bases but have real business experience and contacts in these areas. That is they can find the good contacts easily and their reputation will command respect.

It is also important that you all trust each other.

A team is not a group of people who work together. A team is a group of people who trust each other. Simon Sinek

> ### A Success Story
>
> After the 2007 economic crash, a friend of mine was advised to be ready to cut staff as clients reduced budgets. The cuts came and he was struggling to let the team he had built go. His lady finance director came to him and said
>
> "I know you are struggling with this, let me help you decided who goes and who stays, and tomorrow I will be there and, if you cannot let them go, I will"
>
> My friend knew that he had to speak to the staff face to face and was no longer on his own, he was doing it on behalf of the team, for the good of the team as a whole. The business survived and as the situation stabilised, many of the staff later re-joined the business.

Returning to the teams that run the WHAT and the HOW

Building teams normally involves employing people, which is a commitment requiring the ability to pay them. So far we have looked at:-

1. Your Initial and evolving plan.
2. Customers.
3. Your People.
4. Premises.
5. Cash Flow Management.
6. Marketing.
7. Raising Finance - Getting our Working Capital in Place.

In other words, we have a business that is generating cash, and is ready to scale to the next level.

So the first question is:-

Should you grow your business?

There are certainly risks and many companies choose not to. As long as we drink and wash with water people will always need plumbers! The trouble is that whilst being a plumber will always earn you a living, as a business, it is worth nothing without you. Also in an ever faster changing world, who knows what might come next.

So be flexible, only employ staff when you are confident they will earn you money.

A Success Story

A friend of mine used to tell people how many people he employed, now he tells people that he is turning over £15 million with only 6 employees and that each employee returns 5 times their salary cost.

So just as an exercise:- These are high end people, so say a salary of £100,000 per annum, times 6 employees, times a five-fold return is a £3 million gross profit = 3/15*100% = 20% Gross profit.

So this is probably a high volume but mature market that should be looking for the next product range.

People often say their dream is to have a business that runs itself. I don't think that is realistic. What you can do is to build a business that you run and that someone else can take over and run without you. That is how you take the cash and exit.

Understand the Risks.

How does employing more staff cause problems?

It is generally understood that you can build a business up to 10-20 people yourself, at which point there is a "Glass Ceiling". There is another "Glass Ceiling" around 100 staff.

Why is this? Well you can probably just about manage 10 people on your own. You can maintain a relationship with them and personally manage what they do every day. Some owner managers find it very hard to get to the point where they can let go.

The trick is to start thinking about building teams from the outset, from your first employee.

Problems increase to the square of the number of people until the teams start to perform.

Managing teams of people

1. It is a good idea to think of teams of five people. It has stood the test of time and worked for organisations from the Mafia to the British Army.
    a) Two people argue.
    b) Three is the same - two against one.
    c) Four is- two against two– no decision.
    d) Five people allows for a majority and a mix in the alliances.
2. How will the team work with you? How will you manage them? Think about your business styles.
    a) **The Entrepreneur** - Vision, Staff and Customer Engagement - *Motivation and Sales.*
    b) **The Technician** - Quality Control, Cost Management - *Production Focus.*
    c) **The Manager** - Creating a structure from the entrepreneur's chaos - *Bringing Order and Comfort Zones* (see the e-Myth below).
3. How will you manage your various roles to ensure you are not overly dependent upon one member of staff?

4. Think hard about the mix on the team, what are the expected outputs from the team as a whole. *Who are the Drivers and who are the Doers?*
5. Staff want to feel valued. Their personal status can revolve around doing a good job. They want to know who they are within the team.
6. You mess with the team at your peril! And yet there must be evolution and change. This is the essence of the *Learning Organisation*

> **You need to learn how to manage teams so your business can take on a life of its own.**

How should you build teams of people?

I have a couple of really simple tests to help you decide how to build the team.

The First is the test of Delegation. There are two common realities when it comes to business owners allocating responsibility to others. *Abrogation* and *Delegation*.

Abrogation – It is your problem now! I wash my hands of it! This is often a subconscious attempt by the owner to demonstrate that he is indispensable. The staff member fails, the owner says – *I told you so - If a jobs worth doing, do it yourself etc. etc.*

A number of things just happened.

1. The staff member failed.
2. Every one saw it.
3. The owner made himself indispensable.
4. He made the staff risk averse.
5. The owner stopped the business growing without him.

Arguably the whole point of being in business is to employ people to do the work for you so you can grow the business.

So what is the alternative? - *Delegation*

There are *"Five processes of delegation"*. In my experience, when something goes wrong it is because one of these processes has been missed.

1. This is the Job that needs doing.
2. You are responsible for this job.
3. These are the stages of the job, timescales and outputs at each stage.
4. Repeat back to me the stages, timescales and outputs at each stage.
5. How will you let me know when each stage is completed so I can monitor your progress?

So having been clear about the instructions, and you may need to write them down, you can sit back and see what happens.

This is Test 1

Learn to delegate effectively.

How do you build confidence in your teams?

The Initiative Test - Test 2

Let's say the job has five main stages A through to E. Those who get from A to B before asking for further instructions are AB'ers

My experience is that most people start as AB'ers. They will come back at every stage and ask what to do next. Some will grow into AC'ers and a few into AD' ers.

Those who can jump straight to E don't need you - so watch them. You have to treat these people differently.

According to how quickly staff progress from A through to D; is your selection criteria for your teams.

> **Build confidence in your teams so you can broaden their comfort zones.**

Remember that different people learn in different ways. There is a strong case for face to face training, because often your, most loyal, productive and committed staff are the ones who need help to change. They believe in a certain way of doing things, and will not change because they read a book on the subject. They need hand holding through the change process, until the new process has become a habit.

Who should you have in each team?

If you have five AB'ers that is not a team, it is five individuals that you will have to manage individually. However, with time they will build in confidence by referring to each other, rather than you, and from the group will emerge a spokesman. Make sure they can actually perform the tasks, and are not just blagging it. Then make them the *Team Leader*. Team leader means the person responsible for ensuring the outputs take place on time and to the required standard.

To make that happen they will need to train up the rest of the team, this way they can progress to managing two teams.

> *Use your judgement, watch people interact, see who delivers and who procrastinates.*

"Successful people build each other up. They motivate, inspire, and push each other. Unsuccessful people just hate, blame, and complain." Anon.

How should you reward your best people?

With responsibility comes reward. That reward may come in many forms not just remuneration. Performance related incentives are better than pay rises. A pay rise just becomes the new base line.

Pay rises come as trust is developed in the ability of the individual to grow the teams around them.

> ***Make your best people
> feel special –
> because they are.***

How to build successful teams?

Staff are a mix of people who have good and bad days. The mix of the team is important here. Regardless of their skill levels people are generally either:-

Positive and looking for solutions (S's) or *Negative* and looking for problems (P's)

- Your team will work with 3S's and 2 P's.
- It will fly with 4S's and 1P. In fact they will leave the P behind.
- It won't work with 3P's and 2S's.
- They will drag the team back to 5 AB's that is no team at all.

So you need to be very careful, indeed almost ruthless in finding your first team of 5.

This is why new CEO's often bring their own trusted team with them.

As people come together for the first time you can expect the following:

1. **Forming**   We are all friends together - No basis for Trust.
2. **Storming**   Deciding who does what, why and how – Building Alliances.
3. **Norming**   Learning to work together – Identifying Skills.
4. **Performing**   Supporting each other, doing it well – Trust based on confidence in the skills.

So when everyone falls out with each other, don't panic it is part of the process. Just try to ensure that everyone has a useful role to play.

It is a bit like meetings. When the action points are written up, everyone should have something to do, or there was not much point in being at the meeting, or indeed coming to the next.

Practice building teams, if they are not working - ring the changes.

Having built your first teams - What happens next?

Let's come back to the "*Five processes of delegation*".

The next thing that will happen is that staff will start to build their own little empires and consolidate their comfort zones. They will seek to get paid for doing the same tasks every week. The problem is that in a changing world this will not work. They will become obsolete and so will your business.

The first tell-tale that this is happening is that your team leaders will start to stop informing you of outputs and timings. You will ask and they will be too busy. The next thing that will happen is that quality and delivery times start to slip.

This is why your rewards should be performance based until that trust is built.

Ensure you are informed all the time

What about the review process?

At this point the review process kicks in. We went through the *"Five processes of delegation"* with you. You went through the *"Five processes of delegation"* with the team, this has cost you your bonus. Where did it go wrong? As we have discussed, someone will have short cut one of the *"Five processes of delegation"*. Or if that has not happened then someone needs to leave the company. Identify who and instigate disciplinary procedures.

Remember that your role as the owner of the business is to be the ultimate right of appeal. This is important because the staff need to trust you. Stay one step away from disciplinary procedures. Employ an external consultant if necessary.

As you grow into multiple teams and layers of management, keep your structure as flat as possible.

Eventually you will need increasingly sophisticated systems and management techniques to manage your growing team base. But keep it simple. Build teams of five. When you have five teams of five, find someone to manage the five team leaders, and so on.

The review process is vital. It is where you show two things. That you care and that you are in charge.

Managing people is difficult - What are the guiding lights?

Managing people requires a range of skills and I would say that these are some of the guiding lights

1. Know your subject so people respect your opinion.
2. Recognise and cherish people with more detailed knowledge than yours.
3. Be Modest, Don't control or show off.
4. Try to help other people learn in their own way.

5. Success feels like someone else presenting your ideas as their own.
6. Be a facilitator of other people's growth.
7. Free yourself up to learn about the next opportunity.
8. Be Patient, it takes time for teams to build and trust each other, certainly several months, but not longer.
9. Learn to identify the people that are holding your teams up, if you are paying 50 people, you don't want 2 to stop the other 48 performing.
10. Identify the rotten apples and speak to your HR people to get rid of them before they start effecting the rest of your teams.

Above all follow the following process and you will at least know when and where things are sliding and you can act.

Manage Communications across your organisation:

1. Informed by a Customer Mind-Set.
2. Guided by Customer Insight.
3. Co Creating Value with your Customers.
4. Using the Innovative and Iterative Process.
5. Organising teams around your customers.
6. Test, Measure, Learn, Repeat.

Empower your people to work with your customers and be guided by customer insights into the changing world. Challenge them to build consensus and work together to find shared solutions.

Identify where the process is not working and find out who is not performing and why. Act quickly and decisively. Remember the *Water Wheel* in the introduction to this book. This is a real *Waterwheel scenario,* if you don't act quickly your supporting teams will move you from the GREEN into the RED.

This is a dangerous situation because the more you step in to solve the problem the more plates you spin and the more irritable you will become. Thereby making your people more risk averse.

"Mr Johnston you say? He's available - yes.
But approachable? - Not right now."

A Cautionary Tale

Jaan Timmer CEO Phillips Electronics said "Think the Unthinkable"

His staff did and came up with the best quality Video Recorders. Excellent technology but lacking in Customer Focus. You could not record a movie. The tapes were too short. Sony came along with Sony Betamax, three hour tapes of outstanding quality cost £600 per unit. JVC developed a £300 unit that recorded three hours with pretty good quality and became the industry standard.

People wanted to record movies to a reasonable standard, they did not want to pay double for the extra quality. In fact this is a really good example of where the tech savvy early adopters bought Phillips and then Sony Betamax, but the *Early Majority* could still have video from JVC and feel wise that they had got it for half the price.

The team JVC, who did the least research and incurred the least costs, made the highest gains

Reinvent Yourself

This is about *Customer Focussed Change Management* –

As the world changes increasingly quickly, businesses need to reinvent themselves every three years. This book will hopefully help you survive the next three years, to learn a great deal and build the foundations of a scalable business proposition.

Sources of help

Debbie Glinnan   Parallel HR - http://www.parallelhr.co.uk/

Longmores Employment Team - http://www.longmores-solicitors.co.uk/site/services_business/employment_law/

Visit http://www.welhatchamber.co.uk/thrive-and-survive to access a continually updated web page of useful links.

Further reading

How to Employ your first 20 People – *Debbie Glinnan*

Enlightened Leaders - *Penny Sophocleus*

HBR's 10 Must Reads on Teams - with featured article "The Discipline of Teams," - *Jon R. Katzenbach and Douglas K. Smith*

How to Win Friends and Influence People - *Dale Carnegie*

With Winning in Mind 3rd. Ed. - *Lanny Bassham*

Chapter 9 - Innovation

"This is a wonderful and innovative solution to our problems, but we could never consider it, it's never been done before."

The whole point of innovation is that it involves doing things that have never been done before.

It is important that you identify the people in your business who are blockers and luddites and take them out of decision-making positions. If you don't, you will do all the work to build your business, then find it will fail, because you cannot reinvent yourself.

Innovation is how you deliver a scalable and sustainable business.

Innovation is the Force for Good – The search for a better world.

Innovation it is how you manage your gross profit % by ensuring that your products and services are perceived as cutting edge by your customers.

"The reasonable man adapts himself to the world; the unreasonable one persists in trying to adapt the world to himself. Therefore, all progress depends on the unreasonable man." George Bernard Shaw

"New ways of thinking about familiar things can release new energies and make all manner of things possible." Charles Handy

"Innovation distinguishes between a leader and a follower." Steve Jobs

In England we have 5 of the world's top 10 universities, and we have produced some of the most innovative concepts from Boyle's Law, to the Internet, from the first computer to the discovery of the Higgs Boson, and yet so many of our ideas are developed overseas. I want to help provide a framework where we can protect you from IP theft, and look after your interests throughout the life of your invention. This means understanding the process of innovation.

What is *Innovation*? It is about how you deliver a scalable and sustainable business. It is also where all the concepts we have discussed so far come together. Until now we have looked at a static world, we have considered mainly the present and how you prepare for the future. Innovation is how you take your business into the future, not more of the same but a conveyor belt of products and ideas that will serve a range of markets at different stages of development. This spreads your risk and greatly increases your chances of influencing customer behaviour and hitting the right market at the right time.

Innovation creates a succession of new products awaiting to generate cash like waves arriving on a beach.

The Product GP Lifecycle

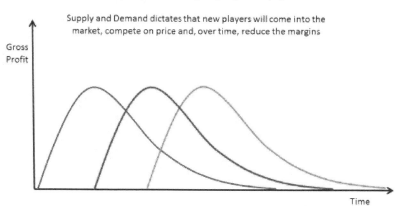

Each product has its time, its "Must Have" moment, when the *Early Adopters* and *Early Majority* are buying.

Supply and Demand dictates that new players will come into the market, compete on price and, over time, reduce the margins

Gross Profit

Time

Innovation:-

- Creates new markets.
- Drives customer aspirations and hence loyalty.
- Inspires staff.
- Ensures your firm survives.

The Three Phases of Communication

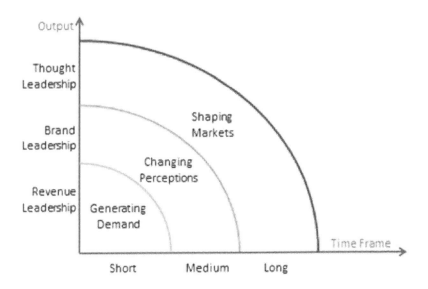

Innovation looks forward to your future products:-

In the short term. **WHAT** you do - is *Generating Demand* and delivering cash flow through the sale of your products today to deliver *Revenue Leadership* (High GP%)

In the Medium term. **HOW** you do it - is building trust and *Changing Perceptions* through customer experience and your understanding the emerging *Customer Needs*, to deliver *Brand Leadership*

In the long term. **WHY** you do it - is creating a shared belief in a better future created by working together with your customers to develop tomorrow's products, thereby *Shaping Markets* through your *Thought Leadership.*

Questions

1. What about the human barriers to innovation?
2. What is your GP% for each product group into each market?
3. For each product group and market, which *Innovation Adoption Phase* are you currently experiencing?
4. How does this impact on your cash flow today?
5. How do you expect this to impact on your cash flow tomorrow?
6. Considering the above, which products should you be selling into which markets?
7. What is *Innovation*? - A more detailed look
8. Which skills will be necessary for success?

Think About

What about the human barriers to innovation?

Think about your staff. How do they learn as individuals? Different people do have different learning styles. I have a nasty habit of talking whilst I am thinking things through. With some people this works because you can explore the options together and develop shared values. Other people especially experts, are really not interested in your opinion, they just want your permission to proceed. (Note to Self!)

A simple "Yes" would
have sufficed!

Quite a lot of people like to go away and research the subject so that, when they speak, they do so with authority. Experts are expected to know after all. The problem being that if you have already decided the answer before the meeting, it is difficult for the team members to have joint ownership and shared values of the way forward. There is a real danger of the team leaving it all to the expert.

I think that most people are comfortable with what they know, asking them to do something different can be a threat. The way forward is to hold people's hands into new territories so they can do it for themselves. When they see they can do it, they will post rationalise the advice, and make it their own. You need to encourage this behaviour to develop team ownership of the WHY, that your staff can develop with your customers. You will then have built a *Learning Organisation* capable of delivering innovation.

"You change the way people think by changing what they do."

What is your Gross Profit % (GP %) for each product group?

List your current range of product groups.

Think about who you sell them to – your Markets.

List them in order of highest to lowest GP% – Your GP% Spread.

Which innovation phase are you currently experiencing?

Take your GP% spread and allocate an innovation phase to each item.

Customer Adoption Phases

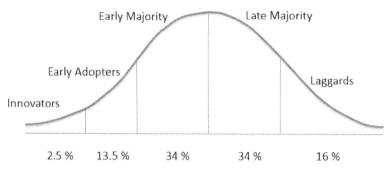

Innovation Adoption Lifecycle

How does this impact on your cash flow today?

Have a look at this sample illustration:

Adoption Phase	Margins % of your highest GP	Sales Volume % of Market Share	Ratio of Expected Cash
Innovators	100	2.5	2.5
Early Adopters	100	13.5	13.5
Early Majority	80	34	27
Late Majority	60	34	20
Laggards	40	16	6.5

These figures are purely illustrative, and need to be completed using your own figures.

The point being that you need to have a feel for which products in which markets are coming on stream in cash flow terms and which are delivering diminishing returns. This will determine where you should be concentrating your marketing efforts.

How will this impact on your cash flow tomorrow?

Remember that those products being sold into existing customers have the advantage of being an established brand. Those markets without a brand presence will require investment to build the brand.

Product Lifecycle:- Sales and Profits

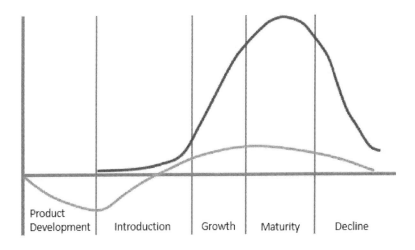

This diagram illustrates the upfront P&L losses and hence cash flow losses you will make, when compared with downstream sales.

Let's look at the different market types in which you might consider building a market presence.

Market Types	Brand Presence	Lead Time	Cash Flow / Working Capital Required
Customer Led Incremental Selling continuously improving existing products to Existing customers	Strong	Short	Small
Customer Led New Markets Selling continuously improving existing products to New customers – e.g. a new region in the same country	Quite Strong	Medium	Medium
Step Change New Markets Selling continuously improving existing products to New customers – e.g. a new country and culture - Export	Weak	Longer	Larger
Step Change New Products Cross-selling new products to New and Existing Customers	Depends You start again with the Early Adopters	Long	Significant

Which products should you be selling into which markets?

Using the format below, list your range of products and collect them into product groups based upon similar GP%'s. In the Existing Markets column write down your existing turnover. In the Future Markets Column write down the turnover based upon market size and expected market share next year. In the income box sum existing and future cash flow. Then considering the GP for each product group you can find the outgoing cash flow. For example, if your existing market turnover for Product A is £500,000 and your GP % is 10%, then you will be adding £450,000 into the Outgoing Cash Flow box and £50,000 into the Net Cash Flow box. When you add in the figures for Future Markets the Cash Flows may well be negative. Add in the time to Breakeven for the future market cash flows into the final column.

Product Groups	Existing Markets	Future Markets	Income Cash Flow	Outgoing Cash Flow	Net Cash Flow	Lead Time to Breakeven
			£ Total	£ Total	£ Total	

This will enable you to consolidate this data into a combined monthly cash flow forecast and see what you can afford to do and when. You can then look at **What If** scenarios.

Let's have a quick look at how the *Working Capital* requirement is effected by the current size of your business and how that compares to your competitors. This is based on the typical company size distribution for a population of 50,000.

What do the Firms Want?
The Innovation Types – A Financial View

Number of Companies	Micro 45,000	Small 4,500	Medium 450	Large 50
Employees	<5	>5 <50	>50 <500	500+
Customer Led Incremental	Generate Cash Minimise Overhead	Marketing & Brand Differentiators	Volume & Scalability Hold up Margins	International Compatibility
Customer Led New Markets	Working Capital	£ Risk Quantification	Market Knowledge and ROI	Global Reach
Step Change New Markets	Partners to Back them	Partners with experience & £	Market Knowledge and ROI	Partnering
Step Change New Products	Partners to Back them	Partners with experience & £	Customer Belief in the Force for Good Majority take-up	Roll out new products quickly

Which skills will be necessary for success?

What do the Firms Want?
The Innovation Types – A Skills View

Number of Companies	Micro 45,000	Small 4,500	Medium 450	Large 50
Employees	<5	>5 <50	>50 <500	500+
Customer Led Incremental	Close Team Commitment Freedom	Marketing and Customer engagement Skills	Volume Channel and Distribution management	Logistics Currency Global Trust Skills
Customer Led New Markets	Sales Team	£ Risk Quantification	Market Knowledge and ROI	Global Reach
Step Change New Markets	Difficult	Partners with experience & £	Market Knowledge and ROI	Partnering
Step Change New Products	Partners to Back them	Partners with experience & £	Customer Belief in the Force for Good Majority take-up	Roll out new products quickly

It may well be that you will need to access additional skills to move into new markets. The skills view above explores some of those considerations. If you are going to hire in skills, you will need to consider the cash flow implications. However, remember that time is of the essence, and this may take longer than partnering with firms with an existing presence in that market, and sharing the profits.

What is *Innovation*?

Ultimately it is how you ensure that your products and services are perceived as cutting edge by your customers.

It is the demonstration that you can deliver against:-

1. **The WHY** - *Your promises to yourself* - **The basis of Belief and Vision**.
2. **The WHAT** - Your promises to your customers - **The basis of Trust.**

3. ***The HOW*** - *Your promises to Staff-* **The basis of Skills and Knowledge Growth**.

It is the *Changing Dynamics* of, and the interactions between, this *Holy Trinity*

Your Beliefs and Visions

Your Customers' Dreams today and

Your Staff and Customer's belief in a better and shared future.

That will deliver a scalable and sustainable business.

These are the pillars upon which you can grow your brand.

The problem is that we live in a changing world and as we have discussed in **Chapter 6 - Marketing**, what is fashionable today will not be fashionable tomorrow, unless you can find new markets.

So we need to identify the types of new markets and the costs / risks / strategies associated with establishing yourself in those markets.

So let's define in very broad terms the 4 types of new markets using mobile phones as an example

1. **Customer Led Incremental** – The customers want bigger screens. You sell incrementally improved products to existing customers
2. **Customer Led New Markets** – As your customers are seen to become fashionable, word of mouth converts new customers to your cause. Consider the growth of the Android phone market. Early Tec. adopters, influenced the early majority, Apple becoming "Looks Good but Tec Old Hat" *Open Source* beating proprietary operating systems.
3. **Step Change New Markets** – This is about mobile phone sales into the third world. The market for second hand phones- the take up of mobiles across Africa is staggering

4. **Step Change New Products** - This is about mobile chip technology in your watch, your glasses, the whole *Internet of Things*. How long will it be before a thought can make a phone call from a chip in your body? And how dangerous would that be??

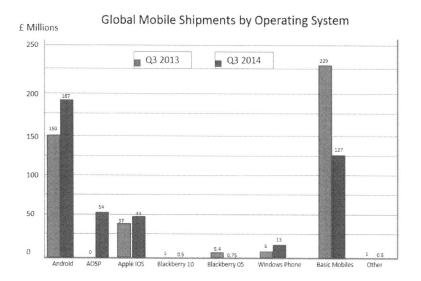

Global Mobile Shipments by Operating System

Interestingly I read today, 30th July 2015, that Samsung are dropping the price on their Android phones, because volume is dropping in China due to the economic slowdown there. Across the world Android has become mainstream and to keep their manufacturing capacity full they are dropping the price to appeal to the *Late Majority* and hence maintain sales volume.

How to Scale the Medium and Large Businesses ?
The Innovation Types - A Customer Led View

Number of Companies	45,000	4,500	450	50
Employees	<5	>5 <50	>50 <500	500+
Customer Led Incremental	Survival	Building Trust	Established	Multiple Market
Customer Led New Markets	Referral	Brand Building	New Products New Markets	Multiple Market
Step Change New Markets	Unusual	New Products Home & Export	Partnering with Smaller Firms	Partnering
Step Change New Products	Tech led University	New Kid on the Block Early Adopter Market	Scaling Early Adopter to Early Majority	With Large & Medium to Late Majority

So here we are looking at the different sizes of business and how the relationship with your customers' changes with each new market opportunity. This approach should help you to think through what is involved in making the change, what it might cost and how long it might take to pay back your investment. The gap is the working capital you will need to finance that change. This is how you start to quantify the risk.

Sources of help

Welwyn Hatfield Chamber of Commerce -
http://www.welhatchamber.co.uk/
nick@welhatchamber.co.uk

Visit http://www.welhatchamber.co.uk/thrive-and-survive to access a continually updated web page of useful links.

Further reading

The Innovator's Dilemma: When New Technologies Cause Great Firms to Fail - *Clayton M. Christensen*

Chapter 10 – Exporting

"Well, Pete and Harry, It looks as if we are going global.
No-one wants our products around here."

We in the UK, live on a tiny Island, the opportunity is in the rest of the world.

Ok so why is exporting included here as part of a business strategy?

The main reason for exporting is that is can give your products a whole new lease of life.

> **Yesterday's products in the UK are tomorrow's products overseas.**

Around the world London is considered to be one of the Great Cities of the World. There is a perception of quality, consistency and trustworthiness that comes from having a stable Government and a free press to maintain that stability – Long may it last.

When it comes to exports our National Brand plays a part. The **WHY UK?** becomes involved. There was a time in living memory when *Made in England* was a by word for quality and Germany was facing hyper-inflation imposed by the French. We are now perceived as a service led rather than manufacturing led country, however there are plenty of opportunities to export. You would not guess it but our biggest export is Jewellery, based upon our design skills and our trusted quality assurance. If we say a diamond is a 2.3 carat, VSI 1 on an F colour, then it will be, because we have an international reputation to protect.

As at 2016 the one way to clear the UK National debt responsibly is via exporting. You pay back international loans by earning the money to do so in international markets – That is *Exporting*.

This means that there are grants available to help you export, there is also *Step Change Funding* available to help you change the course of your business to *Innovate*. That could include a move into exporting.

So I would say that Exporting is a bit like Innovation in the rear view mirror. Innovation is the HOW? The evolving relationship between your staff and customers that delivers new innovative products one after another. The opportunity in exporting is to give those new products that have become tired in your home markets a new lease of life in overseas markets.

You can think of the Innovation Adoption diagram in terms of each line representing a new product arriving in an overseas market like waves arriving on a beach.

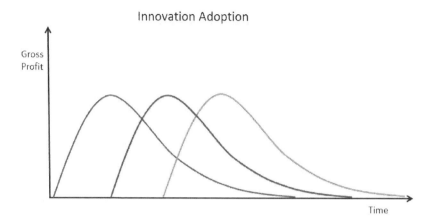

You can then think of those same products arriving in multiple new markets. The point being that you are less concerned about Intellectual property, and GP% in secondary markets, you want to find a *Joint Venture* partner with existing distribution network who can do the legwork whilst you collect the cash-flow.

Questions

1. Why should you export?
2. What are the opportunities to sell overseas?
3. How do you know what they want?
4. How do you access these markets?
5. Why are British firms well placed to export?

Think About

Why should you export?

You should consider exporting because at the time of writing:-

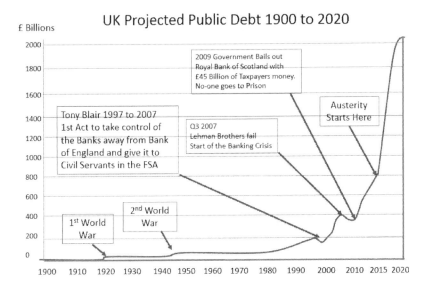

UK Projected Public Debt 1900 to 2020

National debt is at an all-time high. George Osborne the UK Chancellor wants to increase UK exports from £600bn to £1,000bn by 2020. This will only stand a chance if we start to scale medium sized UK firms. This means there are grants and matched funding available to help you succeed.

I have talked about the attraction of spreading your risk across a range of markets, and how this continuously evolving process of innovation can help protect your GP%.

What are the opportunities to sell overseas?

We export a great deal to Europe. We should continue to do so. Can we export more to Europe? Well yes, but it is a competitive market.

How about emerging markets, Malaysia, India, China, Africa?

How do you know what they want?

You have to ask them. (We are working on this)

How do you access these markets?

Consider partnerships with existing exporters.

Why are British firms well placed to export?

Britain is a thought leader in **Language**, **Fashion** and **Quality**. Is there an overseas market that you could sell your, not quite cutting edge, products in the UK into an overseas market where it would still be cutting edge?

Some examples:-

I went to a party in Berlin where the *Birdy Song* was all the rage, ten years after it was in the UK charts.

When the Chinese bought Volvo, sales in China plummeted. Why? Because the Chinese wanted European quality. The Chinese now manufacture in China, ship to Sweden for assembly where Sven signs the paperwork, then ship back to China. Sales have fully recovered. Margins and sales are a product of the perception of quality and exclusivity.

I have a colleague who ships hotel equipment to Nigeria. He imports from China, puts it in a British box and sends it out. The Nigerians know these are Chinese goods but are happy to pay a premium because they get a consistency and quality that allows them to differentiate their hotel group from the competition. When you stay in a hotel a consistent level of service is at the top of the list.

His and other colleagues experience is as follows:-

1. It is well worth speaking to UKTI, they have contacts and sometimes subsidised help.
2. You will find a number of time consuming red tape from HMRC. You just have to identify the rules and get on with it.
3. One of the attractions of Export is that customers are accustomed to paying up front for goods and services prior to shipping.

Sources of help

Welwyn Hatfield Chamber of Commerce -
http://www.welhatchamber.co.uk/
nick@welhatchamber.co.uk

Visit http://www.welhatchamber.co.uk/thrive-and-survive to access a continually updated web page of useful links.

Further reading

Exporting from Failure To Success: An Exclusive Global Guide for Small & Medium Enterprises – *Georgia Lainiotis*

Chapter 11 – Exit Strategy

"My partners and I have discussed your offer, and our knowledge of this market tells us that the valuation should be based upon the sales figures right about here."

"This is important, you need to plan your sale, never run a one horse race"

OK, so this is where all the advice I have given so far comes home to roost. Does the business you have built have sustainable value that someone else is prepared to pay you a significant sum of money for?

So let's look at the stores of value in your business.

The WHY?

You have built a brand that your staff and customers believe in. This means that customers will pay a higher gross profit % for your products than those of your competitors and your staff will go the extra mile because they believe in the vision. This in turn gives focus to team building and helps deliver a *Learning Organisation.*

If a purchaser could acquire your brand and impart those values to their teams, what would it be worth to them to:-

1. Cross sell all their products at a higher margin than they currently achieve?
2. Use your brand credibility in the market to introduce new products into the market that had previously had no existing brand credibility?
3. Use your brand to launch their products into an early adopter market place rather than their existing late majority market?

> It is the difference between success and failure.

What would that mean to them in terms of increased cash flow and future profits?

The WHAT?

What you have now. You have built an existing customer base with a great trading reputation selling at higher GP% than your competitors. You have systems that work and shared values in line with your beliefs that your staff and customers support. Your business runs pretty smoothly without you. Your input is at the review stages overseeing the reports from your managers. You have teams that operate well together, so you have built a *Learning Organisation.*

Your purchaser may well have lower GP%'s than you, and will have a more arms length relationship with customers, so what would it be worth to them to:-

1. Sell their products at your GP %.
2. Acquire your systems that manage your staff / customer interface.

3. Acquire your systems that drive your profitability management.
4. Integrate your customer facing approach into their existing teams
5. Understand your review process, the fairness and the comfort zones created.
6. Be able to create a *Learning Organisation*.

What would that mean in terms of increased cash flow and future profits? Have a look at their Profit and Loss account, and see what these steps would be worth to a prospective purchaser.

The HOW?

The HOW, is your process for delivering a *Sustainable Future*. You have built an organisation that is trusted by its customers because your staff have a relationship with those customers. This relationship makes your staff the guardians of the customers' future needs. This means that your customers will not only pay a premium for your services, buy your incrementally innovative products and help you to de- bug any teething problems, but they will also support you in your step change innovation into completely new products because they believe that they are part of your *Shared and Sustainable Future*.

Conversely, if your purchasers simply do not have this relationship with their customers, then they will be exposed to declining margins and takeover by someone else or eventually to ceasing trading. What would it be worth to them to:-

1. Be future-proofed against declining margins?
2. Have their customers' beta test their products free of charge?
3. Be able to be a pioneer with new product development?
4. To be seen by their peers as a true innovator?
5. What would that mean in terms of future profits and cash flow?
6. What would the premium be to become a real visionary and innovator?

The Owner of the purchasing business may well be an innovative thinker. They just have not had the vehicle to drive there.

There are three key things to get right when selling a business.

1. Understand the potential purchasers' business so you can quantify the value to them.
2. Make sure there are plenty of potential purchasers to compete with each other.
3. The "Deal" is not done until the money is in the bank.

> *Be wary of businesses who want to understand your business and customers for their own gain. Professional managers being a case in point.*

Questions

1. When is the right time to sell?
2. Who will you sell to?
3. Where is the value?
4. Are there any cross selling opportunities?
5. Which sector?
6. What size of business?
7. Cash deal vs shares and cash.
8. Deferred Consideration.
9. What is a *Price / Earnings (P/E) Ratio?*
10. How to get cash out and maintain control?

Think About

When is the right time to sell?

Sell at the top of the market is the obvious answer. Needless to say it is not that simple. Large firms build cash surpluses in the good times with a view to picking up firms cheap in the bad times. There is often a flood of acquisitions as the country comes out of recession. Today we have what looks like a long slow haul out of recession. So I would say the best time is when you are ready.

Who will you sell to?

You should definitely have a plan, be aware of the gaps in your competitors' markets and the desires of your partner firms. Your partners will treat you better than your competitors who will see you as a threat.

> *Have a plan, set up the competition, and hold a Dutch auction.*

Where is the value?

What will people buy? Your brands and reputation, your customer base, the systems and processes you have built up in your business and the employees that use them, your physical *assets, and your cash flow.*

It is worth remembering, that subject to the type of deal reached, your personal involvement may not be wanted or desirable, because of the staff's transfer of loyalties to the new owners. They will have their own vision, and it has to be separate to yours.

Your *Brand* and *Reputation* have a value. We have looked throughout this book at the importance of your reputation to GP%. A firm with a less good reputation can leverage their GP% by acquiring your reputation. Have a look at their accounts and compare their GP% to yours. It is important to understand your potential purchaser's business so you can see where the potential value is to them and negotiate accordingly.

Your customer base, has its own value, but look for companies selling similar but different products into different markets, if they can sell your products to their customers and their products to your customers, that is a win-win scenario.

The skills, if the skills are complementary, it will allow the purchaser to consolidate their position in the market, by delivering one stop shopping. This also has economies of scale that can reduce overhead and increase sales thereby increasing margins.

The physical assets, buildings, plant and machinery are worth a lot more *in situ* generating cash than they are in a fire sale. Again finding complementary but different products helps. If your cash flow is X pa make sure you get a good multiplier on this plus consideration for your other assets.

See *Price / Earnings Ratio and EBITDA below*

Are there any cross selling opportunities?

Again it is important here to understand your purchaser's business to quantify the value of any cross selling opportunities. If there are cross selling opportunities, you can sell both companies products to both sets of customers at an increased price, the customer benefit being the increased convenience of one stop shopping, and decreased costs, delivered by economies of scale.

Which sector?

Well clearly sell to your own sector, but think laterally, if you are a TV cable supplier an energy company might want access to your customer-base to install smart metering, cross sell power and TV bundles, and position themselves as innovative by selling in "The Internet of Things" online control of all things at home from security, let in your neighbour, to heating, to cooking your dinner from the train on the way home.

What size of business?

Consider that smaller businesses are more likely to be competitors, and it will feel more like a takeover. A bigger company will standardise everything, but you can retain more of your identity within that structure. So I think it depends what you want to do. Take the cash and run – sell to the highest bidder. If you want some continued involvement look for a shared belief and vision that you can be part of.

"We don't talk to each other. Our service is terrible and no one is accountable for anything. The last new idea we had was a decade ago. The team in the US are incompetent and overpaid and our monopoly in distribution excludes innovations coming to the market. Do you know what that means? It means that we are finally a global enterprise business!!!!"

Remember bigger companies are often not better, they just have more of a monopoly.

Cash deal vs Shares and cash

Cash is best. It is in your account and you can do what you want with it.

Shares in a public company can be sold and converted to cash.

If there is no market for the shares, you may be stuck. Think about pre-emption rights that give a right of first refusal to named individuals. Is there a valuation formula? Will they have the cash when you want to sell?

If you do a part cash, part shares in the business deal, how do you know that your business will not make all the profits, but those profits are absorbed by losses elsewhere or other by other provisions.

> *Remember Due Diligence cuts in both directions. If you can obtain guarantees or warrantees from the directors.*

Remember that you could take cash, some shares and a profit share from your part of the business, and ongoing business introduced. You can also sell the assets of the business on their own, particularly in a fire sale. If you are in difficulty, beware that a purchaser might string you along, until you go under then purchase the assets from the liquidator at a reduced price.

Deferred Consideration

There may well be a *Deferred Consideration* that is deferred payments that are dependent upon certain things happening after the sale date. For example, there might be a large contract that may or may not renew. If the contract value is included in the purchase price, then the deferred payments would be reduced if the contract was not renewed, conversely the contract was not included in the purchase price then the deferred payments would increase. Another example would be Warranties on performance being breached or exceeded.

With deferred consideration you need to feel confident in the purchaser's ability to pay. What happens if your staff don't like their new employer and all leave? I have seen it happen.

What is a Price / Earnings (P/E) Ratio?

The Price / Earnings ratio is the ratio between the total price paid for the business and the profits or earnings of that business. So if your business sells for £100,000 and has earnings of £10,000 the P/E ratio will be 10.

If a Public Company has issued share capital of 100,000 at £10 per share it is valued at £1,000,000.

If its earnings are £100,000 then the P/E Ratio is 10.

This is normally looked at on a share by share basis.
So for a public company.

P/E Ratio = Market Value per Share / Earnings per Share (EPS)

So trying to turn this into useful information for you. If you know the P/E ratio for your sector, a measure of how attractive a sector is to investors, then you can take your Profit before tax, your earnings, multiple that by the P/E Ratio and get to a valuation of your business.

I have seen P/E Ratio's as high as 19 for Abbot Mead Vickers in the 1990's but numbers are lower today. I often see valuations of businesses of 3 times pre-tax profits. But it does depend upon the sector and the buyer. I heard this month (August 2015) of a Finance House who paid 20 times Pre Tax for a creative services business they wanted.

> **Deep Pockets make for high multiples.**

Incidentally there are a number of expressions around Earnings, Profit before tax (PBT), Cash Flow, Earnings Before Interest Taxation Depreciation and Amortisation (EBITDA), all are measures of the profits generated by your business each year.

So effectively the Price is about the Valuation of the business be that in terms of price paid or the valuation on a stock market.

How to get cash out and maintain control?

Sell on part of your business into new markets. Export markets for example. Find partners with a local presence and sell your products through their distribution network to their customers for a share of the profits.

What are the most tax-effective ways?

Certain assets classes are thought of as chattels, and when you sell them as personal assets the sale is tax free. So for example classic cars and artworks. When interest rates are very low and no one can get a return on their hard earned cash, there is a tendency for them to make markets in these assets. By way of illustration my old DB6 Aston Martin, was great fun for 15 years, but I sold it to pay the wages in 2009. Had I not sold it for the business, but had sold it to myself, for say £35k, I could have sold it today and made £150k tax free. The benefit of hindsight! I knew the day would come. I just could not wait.

Consider joint ventures and profit sharing, then reinvesting profits as a Business Angel. This way you can get a tax relief on capital gains called Entrepreneurs relief.

There are many other things to consider such as management buy outs and buy Ins. These are specialist areas and I would refer you to specialist authors in these areas.

Sources of help

Julian Chapman - http://www.leopardrockcapital.com/

Visit http://www.welhatchamber.co.uk/thrive-and-survive to access a continually updated web page of useful links.

Further reading

The 11 Commandments and 7 Cardinal Sins of Selling a Business - *Robert Goddard*

Chapter 12 – Communities

"We don't have any money left for customer and community engagement, we have spent our budget on social network ads to talk to complete strangers who don't want our products but love IT."

I try to read as much of other people's ideas as I can. It is important to understand the range of opinions and current thinking out there. Understandably people speak from their own experience because that is what they know.

Given the whole spectrum of concepts out there it is not surprising that it can be difficult to see the wood for the trees. This is why I have looked at the growth stages of your business to give you a place to start and some of the tools to build your implementation plan. I hope it helps.

But here is a bigger picture thought process that might start to join up some of the ideas discussed earlier. Let's have a look at what happens in practice.

There are some 50,000 businesses in Hertfordshire, a County due North of London, England, which, for our purposes, will be representative of the UK.

A Community view of UK Businesses

Number of Companies	Micro 45,000	Small 4,500	Medium 450	Large 50
Employees	<5	>5 <50	>50 <500	500+
% of Businesses	90%	9%	0.9%	0.1%
Business Community Type	Family	Extended Family	National Community	International Community
Personal Objectives	Independence + Feed the Family	Independence + Feed Extended Families	Grow wealth beyond the Family needs	Become an International Player
Growth Restraints Tools Required	Owner Led More Customers to build a team	Team led More Skills to build a Brand External Comm's	Multiple Teams More products to build income Internal Comm's	Multiple Divisions Access to multiple markets
Customer Engagement	One to One with Business Owner	One to one with Team	Several to Many with brand values Scalability Model	Many to Many Multiple Brands Acquisition Model
	WHAT	HOW	WHY	WHY

Accepting that this is a vast oversimplification; it is a fact that some 90% of UK businesses are Micro businesses, with less than 5 employees.

This constrains the growth of the business. Typically, the service provided will be a practical one, fix the roof, car or plumbing, walk or wash the dog. This is **The WHAT** of customer Service.

The next bracket of 5 to 50 employees represents 9% of UK businesses. These can be professional partnerships or other organisations who have areas of specialisation that enable them to command a higher Gross Profit in the market. This in turn enables them to employ more people. The organisations feel like an extended family, and are often named after the founder. This extended family gives the organisation shared values and a commitment to learning more. They are constrained by customer growth so the external communications and brand building are at the front of the team's minds. The Customer relationship is still one to one with individuals, you just have different individuals for different skills. The Customer feels part of an extended family, as do the staff. The Customer will purchase specialist knowledge **The HOW** of Customer Service

Less than 1% of the company's employ more than 50 people. Ok it might be 100 people, but it is a small crowd. At this point the business owners do not even know the names of all the people who work for them. So where are the shared values and sense of community? It is here that the internal communications, or *Change Management* techniques become increasingly important. The business has made promises to its customers so it had better deliver against those promises. From the customer perspective their relationship moves from a personal one into a belief in the Brand values of the business. The customers are loyal because they believe in those emotional values; **The WHY** of Customer Service.

The very large companies with over 500 employees have the same problems just in international markets. Often the customers are dealing with the National Division. Their relationship is still with the brand - **The WHY** of Customer Service.

So we return to the Holy Trinity of the *Owners*, the *Staff* and the *Customers* and how the interaction of their relationships determine the success of the business.

The Owner's community

As the owner you have to decide which community you are serving; your family community, your extended family community, a national community or an international community.

You may also want to serve your family or extended family by maximising the value of the business.
If you want to do this, you should start thinking about:

WHY your business is a force for good.

HOW you are going to build a team with the skills capable of engaging with customers to deliver against your promises.

WHAT the customers want in an evolving and ever faster changing world.

In this manner you will develop something that has real value to people who can afford to pay for it.

Understandably most of us start with **WHAT** we have to sell today, and that is why most businesses do not scale and are not sustainable.

So choose the community that matters to you, and remember that the reason **WHY** you do what you do, is to serve that community. **HOW** you do it is how you build your teams and skills. **WHAT** you do is how you pay for it.

> *It's not what you know or who you know that counts, but where you see yourself that matters.*

This is personal to you the owner or shareholder. The business generates the cash to help you reach your goals.

The Staff's community

So as we have discussed, the owners of a business will be thinking in terms of which products satisfy the needs of which customers, and how mature is each market. That is to say - Where is the money coming from?

So as a member of staff you need to think about the types of customer communities you might want to work for. So using a water based trading analogy:

Do you want to be part of a family business, a small boat on an inland lake?

Or part of an extended community, which will require you to gain some specialised skills and sell those skills to customers on a one to one basis, a Ferry, or Coastal steamer carrying knowledge up the coast where you are responsible for your specialist area.

Or would you like to be part of a team running a liner around the Mediterranean, or indeed across the Atlantic.

One of your guiding lights on this might be which Customer Community would you like to be engaging with?

Customer communities

Of course as a customer you are always right and can choose which communities you dabble in.

But, there will be times when you want a personal service to solve a problem.

A time when you will want specialist skills or advice from someone who is a trusted advisor on fashion, or legal matters, and a time when you would like to feel part of something that is important and bigger than you are, something that matters and makes a real difference, a force for good, but you don't want to get personally involved.

You might also want to be part of an evolving community that engages with you, keeps you informed and makes you an authority on the subject amongst your peers.

The emerging village of communities

The fundamental human needs may not have changed but the Internet has opened up an ever expanding range of opportunities for you to join different communities. Here you can express your views, engage, learn or teach others. The range has never been so extensive.

So on the face of it, if you are a business owner, wanting to operate on a national or international basis, or to sell your business to people who already do, then you need to follow the following steps:-

Clearly think through **WHY** your business will help to build a better world.

Work out **HOW** you are going to build teams with the necessary skills to deliver your vision. **HOW** you are going to engage with your customers to be part of their future and a thought leader on their changing needs. So that **WHAT** you do, in the future, is released at the right time, at the start of the GP Curve.

Decide upon **WHAT** it is you are going to do today to pay for it.

Social media is of course one mechanism for managing that interaction.

In this manner you can align the values of your Staff, your Brand and your Customers to deliver a sustainable business.

Sources of help

Visit http://www.welhatchamber.co.uk/thrive-and-survive to access a continually updated web page of useful links.

Further reading

No Excuses!: The Power of Self-Discipline Paperback - *Brian Tracy*

Business and Its Beliefs: The Ideas that Helped Build IBM - *Thomas J. Watson Jr.*

Coda

I hope you have enjoyed reading some of these thoughts, and that they have contributed to your thinking. Business is the game of maximum growth for minimum risk.

I wish you all the very best with your endeavours. Have fun, stay ahead of the curve, avoid the pitfalls, look after you and yours first.

If you would like to share your experiences with me or ask for further help please get in touch on LinkedIn or email me on nick@welhatchamber.co.uk

Nick Brown

Glossary of Terms

Amortisation

> A mechanism for writing off the cost of a building over its useful life. So a £300,000 piece of property may have a useful life of 30 years, so you would write down the asset in the *Balance sheet* with a charge to the *Profit and Loss account* of £10,000 per year.

Aspirational Brands

> We all aspire to a better life for our friends and families, and we like to feel established in our status, so from Cathedrals and Castles, to what we wear on our feet we are all communicating our status. Aspirational Brands help us to spend money to acquire that status. Hence the phrase "To know the price of everything and the value of nothing."

Boiled Frog Syndrome

> The theory is that if you drop a frog into hot water it will jump out sharpish, but if you put him in cold water and bring it to the boil, he will sit there and cook.

Brand Leadership

> Where your brand is considered to be the Brand Leader when compared with competitor Brands. This may be measured by Volume, Gross Profit or Market Share.

Brand Promise

> Your *External Communications,* the promises you make to your customers and staff. The belief in a better future.

Capital Allowances

> Tax relief given for the purchase of Capital Goods, that is Fixed Assets, Plant and Machinery or Equipment for example.

Caveat Emptor

> Let the Buyer Beware, shark infested waters ahead.

Change Management

> The process of keeping your staff up to date on changing *Customer Needs*. You will have this right when your staff are advising you in this area.

Churn

Churn is what happens when you lose existing customers. For example, BSkyB customers cancelling their subscription at the end of the football season.

Cost of Sales

These are costs directly associated with a sale. Costs that would not exist if there were no sales. For this reason, they are also called *Direct Costs.*

Crowdsourcing

Obtaining investment in small amounts from a lot of people over the internet.

Customer Experience

This is what happens when your customers engage with your business. They come full of expectations based upon your advertising and marketing promises that appeal to their *Emotional Aspirations*, then find out the *Rational Reality* when they interact. Customer Experience is increasingly important in a fast changing and *Social World,* because disappointed customers with high expectations will not be kind to you in their chat rooms.

Customer Needs

The current and future aspirations of your customers.

Debt

This is another term for *Loans*.

Deferred Consideration

Any payment that is deferred until after the agreed sales date. These are normally payments that are conditional upon something happening, a contract being confirmed for example.

Depreciation

A mechanism for writing off the cost of an asset over its useful life. So a £30,000 piece of machinery may have a useful life of 5 years, so you would write down the asset in the *Balance sheet* with a charge to the *Profit and Loss account* of £6,000 per year.

Detractors

See *Net Promoter Scores.*

Differentiators

How your customers and staff perceive that your business is different from your competitors, both *Emotionally*, how they feel about your *Brand Promise,* and *Rationally* their *Customer Experience*, what they observe the be the reality of your promises.

Direct Costs

These are costs directly associated with a sale. Costs that would not exist if there were no sales. For this reason, they are also called *Cost of Sales.*

Dividend

The return on Equity or Shares.

Earnings

This is effectively Net Profit, which is Sales, less Direct Costs = Gross Profit less the Overheads = Net Profit.

EBITDA

Pronounced e- bit – da. Is *Earnings* before *Interest*, *Taxation*, *Depreciation* and *Amortisation*. Which translated means your profit adjusted for things that hinder your comparing one company's performance with another's. So one company may be highly *Geared* and hence have higher interest charges, another may be reinvesting profits on machinery and getting *Capital Allowances* that reduce the tax bill, another may have far higher depreciation due to newer machinery, a third might be amortising significant property costs another not.

Emotional Aspirations

This is similar to *Customer Needs.* We aspire to a better world and to be respected by our peers. If we buy an expensive car and it breaks down on the way to the party, then we feel badly let down. The *Customer Experience* is a bad one.

Equity

This is a term for the *Shares* in a business. If you invest in a business by buying shares in that business your return on investment will be paid in a *Dividend*.

Equity Partner

A partner in a business who owns a % of that business as a result of purchasing shares in the business.

Event Horizon

The point of no return. The phrase comes from astronomy, and represents the point at which the gravitational pull from a black hole matches the power of the rocket motors. It is the point beyond which you are converted into atoms and sucked into a parallel Universe.

External Communications

These are the messages you send out to your customers, they represent your emotional appeal to your customers, the Brand Promise against which you will be judged during the *Customer Experience*.

Facilitating Change

This brings us into the realms of change management. The key point is to learn how to help other people to adopt your ideas and make them their own. When your staff and your customers believe that your vision of a better world belongs to them, you will have built a brand with real value.

Fair Market Price

This is often a misleading phrase when quoted by a landlord or his agent. It can mean the highest price that they can find, paid for a different building, in a different location by someone in a different market to yours. *Always do your own research and make an offer you can afford.*

Force for Good

Your Customers Emotional Belief in your business – or otherwise.

Friend

Someone who supports you even when you are in the wrong.

Funding Criteria

The criteria laid out by funders to define who is eligible to receive their funding.

Gearing

The ratio between *Debt* and *Equity* in a business. A highly geared business has a lot of Debt and little equity. This is considered to be a higher risk company because the owners can withdraw their loans (Debt) when they want to. With Equity the cash normally stays in the company.

Given

"A Given" is a brand differentiator that might be expected from someone in your market. So if, as a taxi driver, you claimed proudly that your car had four wheels. That would be expected and would not differentiate your service from your competitors and as such would be *A Given*.

Gross Profit

This is your sales less all your direct costs. That is, those costs that are incurred as a result of the sale - materials, wages etc. Read *How to read a P&L and Balance Sheet* which can be found at http://www.welhatchamber.co.uk/thrive-and-survive.

Gross Profit %

GP% is your gross profit divided by sales, expressed as a %. This is an important number because if your GP% is higher than that of your competitors it is a sign that you customers value your products and services higher than those of your competitors. In short - They trust you and are happy to pay a bit extra.

Growth Stages

Points in your business's development where you take stock of the likely upcoming challenges, see if you are prepared and have the necessary skills, and if not, regroup before proceeding.

Innovation

Innovation implies new ideas that are relevant to your *Customer's Needs*.

Interest

The return on a loan.

Internal Communications

Internal Communications - How you ensure your External Communications, the promises you make to your customers and staff are delivered in the *Customer Experience*. It helps enormously if your staff believe in those promises. *Change Management*.

Internet of Things

A range of products that can be controlled remotely over the internet.

Iterative Process

A process that repeats itself.

Joint Venture

A joint venture is where two businesses go into business together, with an agreement to share profits from the venture. This is distinct from two parties setting up a limited company and sharing profits via dividend distribution.

KPI's

Key Performance Indicators are how you define what you expect your staff to do. They are the outputs from your staff's activities. They are the basis upon which your staff's performance is measured. They are how you ensure that your staff's activities are current and relevant to the changing needs of your customers.

Learning Organisation

An organisation that recognises that being innovative will involve some blind alleys or mistakes, but rather than covering up perceived mistakes, they share the learning and avoid making the same mistake twice. There is also a concept around continuous learning where the things you learned last week are handed on to other staff to free you up to learn some more. This is in contrast to people who learn things, and keep that learning to themselves to justify their existence.

Loans

A loan is an investment in a business that can be recalled at any time. The return on investment is called *Interest*. A loan secured against the assets of a business is called a *Debenture*. If those secured assets are buildings the loan is called a *Mortgage*

Low Margin

Gross Profit % is the Sales less direct costs or Cost of Sales expressed as a % of Sales so a Sale of £125 Direct costs of £100 leaves a gross profit of £25 and 25/125= 20%. Whereas when the Margin on a cost of £100 is £25 than the Margin is 25/100 = 25%. Therefore, a product that is describes is low margin is one with a low mark-up on cost. Therefore, it will also have a low GP%.

Mugged

To be attacked in the street by a group of thugs who were waiting for you and outnumber you. A truly cowardly type of attack.

Net Promoter Score

A number that, for a given *Vertical Market*, compares those customers who would recommend your business to a friend – *Promoters* less those who would not *Passives* and *Detractors*.

Open Source

Code written for the use of all, given freely without licence or charge.

Passives

See *Net Promoter Score*.

Price Elasticity

Price Elasticity is a terms from the field of micro economics that deals with supply and demand. An elastic product is where the price will increase with demand. Gold is a good example. The supply is limited so price rises with demand. An Inelastic product is one where there are plenty of suppliers and putting the price up will result in a drop in demand. A good example might be second hand cars, lots of them, lots of choice, hence the drop in value of a new car when you drive it out of the showroom.

Promoters

See *Net Promoter Score*.

Rates Appeal

The process by which you appeal against your rates assessment for Non Domestic Rates NDR = Business Rates.

Ratings Surveyor

A surveyor who predominantly deals with *Rates Appeals.*

Return on Investment

ROI, is what it says, if you spend £10,000 on a marketing campaign and it delivers £30,000 worth of sales at a GP% of 50% your return will be 30,000*0.50/10,000 = 1.50 or 150%. That is, you get back your original spend plus an extra 50%. Your original £10,000 is spent however, you do not get it back. In the finance world you will expect to get your original investment back. If you invest £1,000 and get £100 back every year, the ROI is 10%. If your investment is by way of a loan, your return is called Interest. If you make an Equity Investment, then you buy shares in a business and your return comes by way of dividends.

Shared Knowledge

This is the knowledge that resides within your teams. It has to do with understanding *Customer Needs* and knowing which team members have the relevant skills and specialisations.

Shared Values

Shared values are where, The WHY you are in business, The WHAT you do to keep your customers happy and HOW you deliver the evolving innovative spirit of your business, all come together.

Shared Vision

The shared ownership of the vision for the business. The WHY, the belief in the Force for Good. The Understanding of the Better World that WHAT you do and HOW you do it, is delivering.

Social World

Before the internet the brands controlled the media, Newspapers, Radio, TV and the customers were excluded. Now your staff and customers have their own media channel. So when they have a bad *Customer Experience* there is a good chance they will tell everyone.

Stalking Horse

In a horse race, a horse designed to distract attention from the intended winner.

Step Change Funding

This is funding aimed at businesses who want to scale their product offering by a significant amount. For example, breaking into new markets.

Target Markets

Target Markets seek to group your full range of customers into niches with whom you would like to engage via a particular media with a particular message.

Thought Leadership

This is where your relationship with your customers is such that they trust you to develop products they have not thought of yet, and buy them to see how they affect their lives. Typically, this will be the Early Adopter Market, but then the others will follow.

Venture Capitalists
People who will invest in your business to take it to the next level. Be wary, they might take it away from you as well.

Vertical Market
A market segmentation time that groups together businesses in the same industry into one vertical market. Useful for competition analysis.

Waterwheel Model
An illustrative model which demonstrates that in business you are either being supported by your friends and colleagues or, you are being dragged under fast.

Working Capital
This is an accounting terms that refers to the liquidity of your business. Read *How to read a P&L and Balance Sheet* which can be found at http://www.welhatchamber.co.uk/thrive-and-survive. It is about your ability to pay your creditors as they fall due. Cash flow can be affected by a number of factors, seasonality, a particular customer paying late, over trading (Taking on extra work that gives you extra staff or stock costs but takes longer to complete and invoice so you get paid later). Working capital is normally supplied by an overdraft facility, which absorbs these troughs then should return to a positive cash position afterwards.

Printed in Great Britain
by Amazon